Past Masters

General Editor Keith Thomas

Wittgenstein

A. C. Grayling is Lecturer in Philosophy at Birkbeck College, London, and Senior Research Fellow at St Anne's College, Oxford. The author of *An Introduction to Philosophical Logic*, *The Refutation of Scepticism*, and *Berkeley: The Central Arguments*, he has also written *Russell* for the Past Masters series.

Past Masters

Forthcoming

A. C. Grayling

Wittgenstein

Oxford   New York
OXFORD UNIVERSITY PRESS

OXFORD
UNIVERSITY PRESS

Great Clarendon Street, Oxford OX2 6DP

Oxford University Press is a department of the University of Oxford.
It furthers the University's objective of excellence in research, scholarship,
and education by publishing worldwide in

Oxford New York

Athens Auckland Bangkok Bogotá Buenos Aires Calcutta
Cape Town Chennai Dar es Salaam Delhi Florence Hong Kong Istanbul
Karachi Kuala Lumpur Madrid Melbourne Mexico City Mumbai
Nairobi Paris São Paulo Singapore Taipei Tokyo Toronto Warsaw

with associated companies in Berlin Ibadan

Oxford is a registered trade mark of Oxford University Press
in the UK and in certain other countries

First published 1988 as an Oxford University Press paperback
Reissued 1996

British Library Cataloguing in Publication Data

Data available

Library of Congress Cataloging in Publication Data

Grayling, A. C.
Wittgenstein.—(Past masters).
1. Wittgenstein, Ludwig, 1889–1951.
I. Title.   II. Series.
B3376.W564G73   1988   192   87-24878

ISBN 0-19-287677-5 (pbk.)

10 9

Printed in Great Britain by
Cox and Wyman Ltd
Reading, Berkshire

Preface

In this brief account of Wittgenstein I aim to do two things. The first is to make clear, for a non-specialist readership, the main outline of Wittgenstein's thought. The second is to describe the place of his thought in twentieth-century analytic philosophy.

Neither of these aims is easy to fulfil in the confines of a short book. There are a number of reasons for this. The main one is that Wittgenstein's writings are numerous, complicated, and obscure. As a result they invite competing interpretations, and have received many. Full justice to Wittgenstein would require a detailed and therefore lengthy examination of his own writings, together with some account of the voluminous literature which has grown around his work. Nothing of the kind can be offered here. My aims, therefore, are modestly conceived. By 'outline' I mean just that; and I assume no prior knowledge of philosophy on the reader's part.

Followers of Wittgenstein argue that it is a mistake to attempt short introductory sketches of his views. One of Wittgenstein's chief disciples, Norman Malcolm, has written: 'An attempt to summarise [Wittgenstein's work] would be neither successful nor useful. Wittgenstein compressed his thoughts to the point where further compression is impossible. What is needed is that they be unfolded and the connections between them traced out.' Wittgenstein's followers add as a further reason the fact that summaries of philosophical views tend naturally to take the form of a systematic account, in the sense of an orderly setting-out of theses point by point, whereas Wittgenstein in his later philosophy expressed an aversion to systematic philosophizing and refused to engage in it. Therefore brief sketches of Wittgenstein's views, his followers say, seriously misrepresent not just their content but their intention.

I am not convinced by these points. Wittgenstein's writings seem to me not only summarizable but in positive need of summary, especially now that they run to a large number of posthumously published volumes containing much overlap and repetition. Nor is it true that Wittgenstein's writings contain no systematically expressible theories, for indeed they do. It is the difference between what Wittgenstein says and the way he says it which is relevant here; the fact that his later writings are unsystematic in style does not mean that they are unsystematic in content. In both his 'early' and 'late' work Wittgenstein puts forward certain key theses, with relations of logical dependence between them, which can be discerned, stated, and explained just as with any philosophical theory. This—briefly and in an introductory way—is what I set out to do here.

The wide latitude for competing interpretations of Wittgenstein nevertheless creates problems. Every commentator tries to give as accurate an account as he can, only to find himself charged with distorting Wittgenstein's views by those who have a different response to them. This might, dismayingly, seem to suggest that there will never be a consensus about what Wittgenstein meant. I do not however think such pessimism warranted, for it seems to me that the literature on Wittgenstein already contains substantial agreement about which themes are most central to his work. This is not to deny that difficulties remain; but it does mean that one can identify with some confidence the aspects of Wittgenstein's work which should be discussed in an introduction like this. Like anyone writing about Wittgenstein, however, I must, to be properly cautious, add that the views I attribute to him are what *I* interpret those views to be; the qualification 'as I read him, Wittgenstein means . . .' should therefore be understood throughout.

The second of the two aims mentioned above is less difficult to attain. It is to situate Wittgenstein's work in twentieth-century analytic philosophy. This is a narrow aim, for it is not at all the same thing as situating his work in twentieth-century *thought* in general. To relate Wittgenstein's ideas to currents in literature and art, or to speculate whether, say, his early work is 'modernist' and his late work 'post-modernist', or to search for the wellsprings of his philosophy in the intellectual ferment of pre-1914 Vienna—this is not the task I set myself in what follows. Such a task would be interesting and in many ways valuable, but here I fasten upon what is immediately relevant only. Wittgenstein's work, considered strictly in its philosophical aspects, is in general taken to belong to the mainstream of recent and contemporary analytic philosophy. It is in this setting that I discuss it.

It should, however, be mentioned that Wittgenstein's name, and occasionally one or other of his ideas, also appears in writings on anthropology, theology, literary theory, and other subjects. Philosophers in continental Europe, whose recent traditions of thought are rather different from those in the English-speaking analytic tradition, have likewise come to pay attention to Wittgenstein's work. A detailed study might take these wider considerations into account. But here, as remarked, I concentrate on Wittgenstein's thought in its primary setting. Judging whether any value attaches to the use made of it in these other spheres in any case depends on first understanding the ideas themselves. Nevertheless, here and there I point out connections with other fields; this happens mainly in discussion of Wittgenstein's later views.

Exposition and explanation take more room than criticism in what follows. This is because space is limited and my primary task is to make the main aspects of Wittgenstein's thought accessible to non-philosophers. It is, however, part of such a proceeding to indicate what critical responses have been evoked by a thinker's views, and to provide some indication of the degree to which those views are persuasive or otherwise, and why. Accordingly I make some brief and untechnical forays in this direction.

In discussing the relation between Wittgenstein's work and other twentieth-century analytic philosophy I offer minor revisions to the standard view, my suggestion being that Wittgenstein's place in recent philosophy—in terms of his actual effect upon its content and direction—is not quite what it is usually said to be.

Introductory books should encourage their readers to investigate at first hand the subjects with which they deal. In some cases, however, it is simply too ambitious to expect non-specialist readers to do this without first acquiring a substantial minimum of background knowledge. Wittgenstein is such a case. Despite claims by his followers to the contrary, he is very much a philosopher's philosopher. His writings, like those of Aristotle, Kant, and certain others, cannot be read with profit by someone who does not have at least a modest grounding in philosophy, for their *point* would be wholly obscure to someone who did not recognize what was being argued for and against. Since this account assumes no philosophical training on the reader's part, I have tried to make it self-contained; the aim is to give a sketch of Wittgenstein's thought which will be informative even to someone who is not, and does not intend to become, a student of philosophy in any systematic sense. Nevertheless, if what follows succeeds in prompting some of its readers to tackle Wittgenstein's own writings, and to do so with greater understanding, that will be a major gain.

My thanks go to Anthony Kenny, Anthony Quinton, Jim Hopkins, Dan Rashid, Henry Hardy, and Keith Thomas for reading the entire manuscript and making valuable comments and criticisms; and to Carolyn Wilde and Norman Malcolm for helpful discussion of certain points in the *Investigations*. The usual constraints and exigencies dictated the outcome, but these advisers ameliorated it, and I am grateful to them.

This is dedicated to Jenny—'*Invenio sine vertice aquas, sine murmure euntes, perspicuas ad humum.*'

Oxford, 1987

Contents

Note on references

The most frequent references to Wittgenstein's works are effected by the following abbreviations:

B   *The Blue and Brown Books*
C   *On Certainty*
P   *Philosophical Investigations*
R   *Remarks on the Foundations of Mathematics*
T   *Tractatus Logico-Philosophicus*
Z   *Zettel*

Numbers following these abbreviations refer to paragraphs, except in the case of B, for which page numbers are given. All other references are explained in the section on further reading.

1 Life and character

Ludwig Wittgenstein was a philosopher. Philosophy in the twentieth century has become a pursuit for specialists, and accordingly most philosophers who have recently acquired reputations are famous only among their fellows. Wittgenstein, however, is famous far beyond the boundaries of philosophy. Among non-philosophers his name is mentioned surprisingly often and in a surprising variety of connections. It seems that by many he is regarded as quintessentially representative of twentieth-century philosophy, as if he exemplifies—not just in his work but in his personality—what philosophy itself is like: difficult and profound. Perhaps for this reason his writings are plundered for aphorisms. They lend themselves to that treatment because of their style and structure, and because they seem to distil something of wisdom.

The layman's estimation of Wittgenstein derives from the fact that many contemporary philosophers think he is the twentieth century's greatest thinker. Whether or not that is true remains for history to decide; the judgement of peers is not infallible. Whatever the decision is, however, it will not alter the fact that Wittgenstein's life and thought were, at very least, extraordinary.

Ludwig Josef Johann Wittgenstein was born in Vienna on 26 April 1889, the youngest in a family of eight children. His father was an industrialist, and one of the richest men in Austria; the Wittgensteins' home was a centre of Viennese social and cultural life.

Wealth and culture had characterized both sides of Wittgenstein's family for several generations. His paternal grandfather was a wealthy Jewish wool-merchant from Hesse who had converted to Protestant Christianity and married the daughter of a Viennese banker. Soon afterwards he transferred his business headquarters to Vienna, where he and his wife established themselves as patrons of the arts. They gave their son Karl, Ludwig Wittgenstein's father, an expensive classical

1

education, but Karl rebelled and at the age of 17 ran away to America, where for two years he lived by waiting at table and giving violin and German lessons. On his return to Vienna he studied engineering. Within decades he had added a fortune to his inheritance by successful involvement in the iron and steel industry, establishing himself as one of the foremost industrialists of the Austro-Hungarian Empire. He was able to retire in his early fifties, and devoted part of his time thereafter to publishing articles on economics in the Viennese press.

It was Wittgenstein's mother Leopoldine who did most to encourage the family's cultural and musical activities. She too was a banker's daughter, with connections among the Styrian landed gentry. Her musical interests were particularly strong. At her invitation Brahms and Mahler were regular visitors to the house, and with her encouragement Wittgenstein's brother Paul became a concert pianist. Ravel and Strauss were among those who wrote one-handed concertos for Paul after his loss of an arm in the 1914–18 war. Wittgenstein himself was gifted with a fine musical sensibility. In adult life he taught himself to play the clarinet, but his most striking musical talent was the ability to whistle entire scores from memory.

Leopoldine Wittgenstein was a Roman Catholic and Wittgenstein was therefore brought up in that persuasion. Religion remained a powerful theme throughout his life; on several occasions he seriously contemplated becoming a monk. His religious sentiments were unorthodox, however, and he kept their exact nature a secret. Hints of them appear in his writings.

Perhaps because of his own experiences Karl Wittgenstein's views on education were idiosyncratic. He had all his children taught at home, to a curriculum of his own devising, until they were 14 years old. The plan was not a success. When the time came for Wittgenstein to attend school he could not get into a *Gymnasium* (the equivalent of a grammar school) or even a *Realschule* (the equivalent of a secondary modern) in Vienna, because he had not attained the required standard. Eventually he passed the entrance examinations for a provincial *Realschule*, in Linz, where his exact contemporary Adolf Hitler was also a pupil. He spent three unhappy years there, leaving in 1906 without the qualifications for university entrance. This was a setback because he had conceived an ambition to study physics with Boltzmann in Vienna. However, he had always shown an aptitude for engineering, his father's profession; it is said that he demonstrated this in childhood by constructing a working model of a sewing-machine. His parents accordingly sent him to a technical college in Berlin–Charlottenburg.

Wittgenstein was not happy there either and left after three terms. He had, however, developed an interest in aeronautical engineering, then the newest branch of his prospective profession. He went to England in 1908 and spent the summer flying experimental kites at the Upper Atmosphere Research Station near Glossop in Derbyshire. In the autumn he entered as a student of aeronautical engineering at Manchester University.

Wittgenstein remained on the register at Manchester for two years, although for most of that time he was in Europe. By the end of his stay he was working on the design of a propeller with jet-reaction nozzles at the tips of its blades. He became intrigued by the mathematics of the design, then by mathematics itself, and finally by philosophical questions about the foundations of mathematics. He asked acquaintances what he could read on this subject, and was directed to Bertrand Russell's *Principles of Mathematics*. The impact of this book on Wittgenstein was great. Hitherto his philosophical reading had been limited; he had read some of Schopenhauer's work but little besides. Russell's book introduced him to the latest developments in logic and philosophy, developments for which Russell himself and Gottlob Frege were responsible. Wittgenstein was excited by these ideas and decided to study them. In 1911 he contacted Frege at Jena University to show him an essay he had written and to seek his guidance. Frege advised him to study with Russell at Cambridge. Early in 1912, accordingly, Wittgenstein arrived in Cambridge and registered as a student.

Wittgenstein spent a mere five terms at Cambridge. Nevertheless it was an immensely formative time for him. He discussed logic and philosophy with Russell, who in a letter written at the time said of him '[he is] the ablest person I have come across since Moore'. The relationship between

Wittgenstein and Russell quickly ceased to be that of pupil and teacher, and although Wittgenstein's friend David Pinsent remarked in his diary 'it is obvious that Wittgenstein is one of Russell's disciples and owes enormously to him', the influence was not all one-sided, as we shall later see.

Travel interested Wittgenstein greatly. In 1913, with Pinsent, he visited first Iceland and then Norway. He was attracted by Norway and returned later in 1913 on his own. In a remote corner of a farm near Skjolden he built himself a hut, and remained there, apart from a short visit to Vienna for Christmas, until the summer of 1914. He devoted his time to research in logic. G. E. Moore came on a visit, and while there took notes of some of Wittgenstein's work. This work represented the earliest phase of progress towards Wittgenstein's first book, the *Tractatus Logico-Philosophicus*.

When war broke out in 1914 Wittgenstein was at home in Vienna. Within a few days he had enlisted in the Imperial army. For most of the next two years he served as a mechanic with an artillery workshop unit on the Eastern Front, first in Cracow and then near Lwow. In 1916 he was sent to Olmütz for officer training. While there he met Paul Engelmann, and they discussed religion together; Engelmann subsequently published a record of their friendship which shows how much significance religious questions had for Wittgenstein at that time.

Wittgenstein rejoined his regiment in 1917 and served as an artillery observer. Early in 1918 he was posted to a mountain artillery regiment in the Tyrol on the southern front. When in November the Austro–Hungarian war effort collapsed, most of the Imperial army in the south, Wittgenstein included, was taken into captivity by the Italians. Wittgenstein remained a prisoner near Monte Cassino until the later part of 1919.

The war had a significant effect on Wittgenstein in at least two ways. One was that it caused in him a profound change of personal outlook, particularly in connection with possessions and manner of life. Before the war he had been left a substantial fortune by his father. Prior to that he had lived as one might expect a generous millionaire's son to live. For example, it is reported that when one day he missed a train from Manchester to Liverpool he promptly set about trying to hire a private train, at that time something one could do if rich enough. Again, Pinsent records that on their trip to Iceland (for which Wittgenstein paid) they travelled so royally and with such a long train of attendants that they attracted the sardonic notice of other tourists. And it seems that before the war Wittgenstein was scrupulous in his choice of neckties. All this changed. Wittgenstein gave the whole of his fortune to his siblings—he took the view that since they were already rich more money would not corrupt them—and thenceforth lived with complete simplicity and lack of ornament, among other things rarely if ever again wearing a necktie.

The reasons for the change are not wholly clear. Possibly they relate to the fact that on the eastern front, at some time during the first half of 1915, Wittgenstein acquired and read Tolstoy's account of the Gospels—*The Gospels in Brief*—and was profoundly moved by it. (It seems that later, when he read the Gospels themselves and found them to be somewhat different, he had to be persuaded of their superiority over the Tolstoy version.) Also it may have been that the austerity and simplicity of army life proved congenial to him; he had shown traces of ascetic inclination before the war, as his Norwegian solitude suggests, and the experience of army ways may have confirmed that predilection. In any case Wittgenstein's letters and recorded conversations show that he had a dark sense of what he took to be his own sinfulness, perhaps because of his homosexuality, and in consequence he was given to self-mortification. Whatever the reasons, when Wittgenstein left the prisoner-of-war camp in 1919 he had recognizably become the unusual, even eccentric, often prickly individual whose later years are so well described by the chief memoirists.

The second matter of significance was that when Wittgenstein was taken prisoner he had in his knapsack the manuscript of his book, the *Logische–Philosophische Abhandlung*, known to its English-language readers as the *Tractatus Logico–Philosophicus* (a name suggested for it by Moore in imitation of Spinoza's *Tractatus Theologico–Politicus*). Wittgenstein had been working on it throughout the war years, and it came to completion in the Monte Cassino camp, where by good fortune he met someone interested in logic with whom he could discuss his ideas.

During the early part of 1919 Wittgenstein managed to send letters to Russell from Italy, telling him of the *Tractatus*'s existence and even, through the influence of John Maynard Keynes, getting a copy of the manuscript to him. After his release Wittgenstein made a number of attempts to have the book published, all unsuccessful. In despair he left the matter to Russell, who eventually arranged publication by agreeing to contribute an introduction. The *Tractatus* appeared in German in 1921 and in English translation in 1922. When Wittgenstein saw Russell's introduction he was angry, complaining that even though he and Russell had discussed the book line by line at a meeting in Holland in late 1919, Russell had misunderstood his views and misrepresented them.

The *Tractatus* was the only philosophical book Wittgenstein published in his lifetime. When it was finished he thought he had solved all the problems of philosophy, and consistently with that view gave up philosophical work and turned his attention elsewhere. He had decided while imprisoned to become a schoolteacher, and quickly put this decision into effect. He took a one-year course in primary school teaching, graduating in July 1920. That autumn he commenced as schoolmaster in Trattenbach, a village in the hills south of Vienna. He spent two increasingly unhappy years there before transferring to Puchberg-am-Schneeberg. Here as at his first post friction arose between Wittgenstein and some of the parents of his pupils, and within two years he transferred again, this time to Otterthal. While there he wrote and published a pronouncing dictionary for use in primary schools. Yet again trouble arose with parents; it seems that Wittgenstein's temper and the alleged severity of his disciplinary methods caused complaints. In April 1926, before official action could be taken over the complaints, Wittgenstein resigned and returned to Vienna.

The failure of his schoolmastering career depressed Wittgenstein intensely. He took a job as a gardener at a monastery in Hütteldorf outside Vienna, and for the third time contemplated becoming a monk (the first was just before the

Great War, the second after his release from prison camp). He went so far as to make enquiries about joining an order; at the interview he was advised that his motives for wishing to become a monk were inappropriate ones, and that he would not find in monastic life what he sought.

From this despairing state Wittgenstein was rescued by two developments. One was that he became increasingly involved in the design and construction of a house for one of his sisters. At first he worked in collaboration with the architect, who was his friend Paul Engelmann, but soon assumed full control. Every detail of the house received his painstaking attention; heating radiators, for example, had to be exactly positioned in order not to disturb the symmetry of the rooms. From some the house has evoked high praise; in the opinion of G. H. von Wright it has the same 'static beauty' as the *Tractatus*. It is a building in an unornamented modern style, influenced by the work of Adolf Loos whom Wittgenstein admired.

The excursion into house building did much to restore Wittgenstein after his difficulties, and it disposed him favourably to the second development, which was that philosophers at Vienna University contacted him and invited him to have discussions. Wittgenstein agreed, and in consequence began slowly to resume philosophical work. He had in fact been in touch with philosophy during his schoolmastering years through the medium of a young English philosopher, F. P. Ramsey, who had assisted in making the English translation of the *Tractatus*, and who visited Wittgenstein in Austria on a number of occasions. But although Wittgenstein discussed the *Tractatus* with Ramsey in some detail he could not be persuaded by him to take up philosophy again. Now, however, he was sought out by Moritz Schlick, professor at Vienna University and founder of the 'Vienna Circle', an active group of philosophers and scientists who worked closely together from 1925 onwards. Schlick did not succeed in drawing Wittgenstein into the Circle itself, but he and various of his colleagues met Wittgenstein on an occasional basis. As Wittgenstein's philosophical interests revived he saw that his *Tractatus* did not, after all, solve the problems of philosophy. This was the stimulus to the development of his second and in many ways quite different phase of philosophical work.

An important result of Wittgenstein's contacts with Schlick and others of the Circle was his return to Cambridge in 1929. He had discovered that he could submit the *Tractatus* for the degree of Ph.D. after one further year's residence. He duly registered, with Ramsey as his supervisor and Russell and Moore as his examiners. Moore, who with others of the older generation disliked the Ph.D. degree, then a new import from the United States, is said to have written in his examiner's report: 'The *Tractatus* is a work of genius, but it otherwise satisfies the requirements for a Ph.D.' After the award of his degree Wittgenstein set about securing a position at Cambridge. He applied for a five-year Fellowship at Trinity College, and with Russell's generous help, given in a report to the college on Wittgenstein's research proposals, was awarded it in 1930. He now entered upon his most fertile and productive philosophical phase, in which he wrote copiously.

When his Fellowship was drawing to a close Wittgenstein decided to emigrate to the Soviet Union, then enjoying a certain vogue in Cambridge circles. As a passionate admirer of Tolstoy and Dostoevsky he had in any case long nourished an admiration for Russia. Accordingly he learned Russian and in 1935 visited the USSR with a friend. It is not clear why he reversed his decision to settle there, but after a year in his hut in Norway, he returned to Cambridge and in 1939 succeeded Moore as Professor of Philosophy. Before he could begin his professorial duties war broke out. Until 1944 Wittgenstein worked as a porter first at Guy's Hospital in London and then at the Royal Victoria Infirmary in Newcastle upon Tyne. He had taken British nationality and was therefore not subject to internment.

In the two academic years 1945/6 and 1946/7 Wittgenstein lectured in Cambridge. Life as a don was highly distasteful to him, particularly in its detail; he found, for example, High Table conversation so disagreeable that he avoided dining there. At the end of 1947 he resigned his Chair and went to Ireland, living for part of the time in a cabin on the Galway coast and later in a Dublin hotel. Here he completed the major work of his later philosophy, the *Philosophical Investigations*.

His health was poor; after a short visit to the United States in 1949 he discovered that he had cancer. From then until his death in 1951 he lived with various friends in Oxford and Cambridge. He continued to make notes of his philosophical ideas, whenever his health permitted, until close to the end.

There are vivid portraits of Wittgenstein in memoirs and reminiscences. Most of these were written by people much influenced by Wittgenstein, and consequently do not offer impartial views of him. Nevertheless, when taken together with the few more objective depictions which exist, and Wittgenstein's own letters, they provide a dramatic picture of the man and his character. In them Wittgenstein appears as a powerful, restless, dominant individual, an intense and complicated man, to whom people responded either with adulation or aversion. The chief memoirists came to know Wittgenstein when they were young students and he was nearing 50 years of age, which may in part explain their hero-worship. They describe him as about 5 feet 6 inches tall, with a transfixing gaze and a fierce, uncompromising manner. Almost everyone who has left a record of encounters with Wittgenstein comments on the power of his personality, and mentions the way people fell under his spell as if mesmerized by the intensity of his expression and the striking gestures he made when discoursing.

Wittgenstein taught by thinking aloud before a group of students in his rooms at Trinity. They knew him to be famous because of the *Tractatus*, yet during those seminars he was repudiating many of that book's central tenets and working out a series of new philosophical ideas in their place. They therefore felt they were witnesses to something important. And not just important but dramatic; it was Wittgenstein's style of teaching to struggle with his problems before them, at times crying out 'I'm stupid today!' and at other times sitting in intense, prolonged silences. Remarks from students, if they did not meet his approval, evoked crushing replies. The ordeal of Wittgenstein's classes did not suit everyone's taste, but so profound an impression did they leave on some that they were

9

unable to think of philosophy in any but Wittgenstein's way thereafter.

The picture of Wittgenstein which has him seated in a deckchair in his sparsely furnished Trinity rooms, conducting his classes in the manner just described, is in a way an unrepresentative one, for Wittgenstein spent only a small part of his life teaching in Cambridge. He was, in truth, a nomad, a rootless wanderer, trailing from one country to another and one place to another, varying longer stays with many restless shorter travels, living alone except when visiting or journeying with friends. His sojourns in one place rarely lasted more than a few years. This was paralleled by the number of different occupations which circumstance or his own choice led him to take up: student, soldier, primary school teacher, gardener, architect, gypsy, don—none of which appears to have given him satisfaction. His was therefore a fragmented and displaced life, and, it seems, not often or for long a happy one.

To some people Wittgenstein showed kindness. Before the 1914–18 war he made an anonymous and generous gift of money to two poets. He was capable of close friendships, and although he was fiercely demanding as a friend most of those who had this relation to him became deeply attached and loyal. He had some particularly close relationships with several of his pupils. To others, however, Wittgenstein could be cruel and dismissive. Some memoirists—those who are not disciples—speak of him as capable of arrogance, intolerance, and rudeness. He caused anxiety among the families of some of his pupils because of the strength of his sway over them. He always sought to discourage people from pursuing academic careers; several gifted pupils abandoned philosophy at his insistence, one of them—to Wittgenstein's satisfaction—spending the rest of his life employed in a canning factory.

One neglected consideration which may go towards an understanding both of Wittgenstein's character and of his philosophy is the nature of his formal education. The sketch given of it above shows that after being taught at home under his father's eccentric regime he had three years at school followed by short stays at various institutions, ranging from a Berlin technical college to Cambridge University. Apart from his teacher's certificate Wittgenstein's only academic qualification was the Cambridge Ph.D., gained at the age of forty. He was by no means a scholar; he did not study the classic philosophers carefully (most of them he did not study at all) and he actively discouraged his students from doing so.

In contrast to this scattered and piecemeal education there is the fact that Wittgenstein's early years were spent in a highly cultured home. In addition to musical interests he acquired several languages, and later added others—Latin, Norwegian and Russian. Undoubtedly he took an interest as a young man in the flourishing intellectual life of Vienna. An indication of this is that he read some of Schopenhauer's philosophy, then fashionable among Viennese intellectuals and artists (one of Mahler's gifts to the young Bruno Walter was a complete set of Schopenhauer's works). This mixture, with on the one hand Wittgenstein's fragmentary formal education and on the other his cultured and patrician home background, may in some part explain the unusual character of his mind and interests. Perhaps unorthodox educations foster originality; or it may be that native originality is stifled by too much formal schooling. Whatever the case, Wittgenstein was not the product of a typical education, and the character of his work bears testimony to that fact. It gives him another distinction: he may well be the last considerable figure in philosophy not to have followed a strict and orthodox academic regime as a condition of being taken seriously by the philosophical community.

2 The early philosophy

In this chapter I discuss Wittgenstein's early philosophical work, the *Tractatus Logico-Philosophicus*. An appreciation of the main doctrines of this book makes Wittgenstein's later philosophy much easier to understand.

Sections 2 and 3 are devoted to the *Tractatus* itself. Section 1 contains an explanation of several background matters which help to make the *Tractatus* more intelligible. The chapter ends with some remarks on the influence of Wittgenstein's early work on other philosophers (section 4).

The scene-setting in section 1, although intended to be a general preparation for discussion of the *Tractatus*, is particularly addressed to those who are quite new to philosophy. It contains an account of certain technical conceptions in logic and philosophy which play an important part in Wittgenstein's early thought. I have set these out in a straightforward way.

1 *Aims and background*

Wittgenstein's aim in the *Tractatus* is stated in its Preface. It is to show that the problems of philosophy can be solved by coming to a proper understanding of how language works. He puts this by saying that we shall solve the problems of philosophy when we understand 'the logic of our language' (T, pp. 3–4). This, indeed, is the dominating thought in all Wittgenstein's philosophy, and it represents what is continuous between its earlier and later phases. As we shall see, however, Wittgenstein's views about 'the logic of language' differ markedly in these two phases, with the later taking as its basis a repudiation of some of the earlier phase's most central themes.

There are two aspects to Wittgenstein's aim as just stated. His objective is *to solve the problems of philosophy*, and he intends to do so *by showing how language works*. Why an understanding of language should 'solve the problems of philosophy' is what the *Tractatus* sets out to demonstrate—as does, in its different way, his later philosophy also. We turn to that demonstration shortly. First, it is necessary to see what is meant by the phrase 'the problems of philosophy'.

One can describe philosophy as the attempt to make clear, and if possible to answer, a range of fundamental and puzzling questions which arise when, in a general and inclusive way, we try to understand ourselves and the universe we inhabit. Among many other things these questions concern existence and reality, knowledge and belief, reason and reasoning, truth, meaning, and value both ethical and aesthetic. The questions themselves are of the form: what is reality? What kinds of things ultimately exist? What is knowledge, and how do we come by it? How can we be sure that our claims to knowledge are not in some systematic way mistaken? What are the canons of correct reasoning? What is morally the right way to live and act, and why?

Philosophical problems are not problems which can be solved by empirical means—by looking through a telescope or microscope, or by conducting experiments in a laboratory. They are conceptual and logical problems, requiring conceptual and logical investigation. Over the millennia a great investment of genius has been brought to the task of clarifying and answering the questions of philosophy. Some philosophers have attempted to construct explanatory theories, occasionally very elaborate and ambitious in scope; others have tried to clarify and resolve particular questions by painstaking analysis and criticism. Almost all those who have contributed to philosophy throughout its history have agreed that the matters mentioned above—existence, knowledge, truth, value—are deeply important; and it is upon this consensus that the philosophical debate, which has gone on at least since classical antiquity, has been based.

Wittgenstein runs against this current. His view is that the proper task of philosophy is not one of engagement with the issues mentioned, for in his opinion they involve illusory problems which arise as a result of misunderstandings about language. The *proper* task of philosophy, he says, is to make the nature of our thought and talk clear, for then the traditional problems of philosophy will be recognized as spurious and will accordingly vanish. Wittgenstein's work—both his early work as embodied in the *Tractatus* and his later work—is dedicated to 'solving' the traditional problems of philosophy in this way.

What is fundamental to the *Tractatus* is the thought that language has an underlying logical structure, an understanding of which shows the limits of what can clearly and meaningfully be said. The importance of this, in Wittgenstein's view, is that what can be *said* is the same as what can be *thought*; so that once one has grasped the nature of language, and therefore of what can clearly and significantly be thought, one has shown the limit beyond which language and thought become nonsense. It is in this realm, beyond the boundaries of sense, where in Wittgenstein's opinion traditional philosophical problems arise, and where their arising is precisely the result of our trying to say what is unsayable—the same, in his view, as trying to think the unthinkable. He puts this point at both the beginning and the end of the *Tractatus* in the now famous assertion that 'what can be said at all can be said clearly, and what we cannot talk about we must consign to silence' (T, p. 3 and cf. T 7). Wittgenstein gives the claim fuller expression in a letter to Russell: 'The main point [of the *Tractatus*] is the theory of what can be expressed by propositions—i.e. by language—(and, which comes to the same thing, what can be *thought*) and what can not be expressed by propositions, but only shown; which, I believe, is the cardinal problem of philosophy.'

The issue of these claims for Wittgenstein is that the proper task of philosophy is 'to say nothing except what can be said, i.e. the propositions of natural science—i.e. something that has nothing to do with philosophy—and then, whenever someone else wanted to say something metaphysical, to demonstrate to him that he had failed to give a meaning to certain signs in his propositions' (T 6.53). But this negative result is not the whole story, for in Wittgenstein's view such matters as ethics and aesthetics, religion, and the 'problems of life' (T 6.52) are not themselves ruled out as nonsensical; it is only the attempt to *say* anything about them which is so: 'There are, indeed, things that cannot be put into words. They *make themselves manifest*. They are what is mystical' (T 6.522). Here 'showing' rather than 'saying' is all that is possible. Sometimes Wittgenstein speaks of the 'more important unwritten second half' of the *Tractatus*, meaning by this that the truly significant issues are identified by what the *Tractatus* does *not* say, for the *Tractatus* shows from within the limits of language what is important. In another letter he says 'For the Ethical is delimited from within, as it were, by my book . . . All of what *many* are *babbling* today, I have defined in my book by remaining silent about it.'

The task Wittgenstein sets himself in the *Tractatus* is therefore to explain, with a view to establishing the foregoing points, how language works. More specifically, his task is to reveal the nature of language and its relation to the world, which in effect amounts to explaining how meaning attaches to the propositions we assert. Accordingly he devotes the major part of his attention in the *Tractatus* to describing what propositions are and in what their meaning consists. And this, for Wittgenstein, is as we have seen the same as identifying the limits of *thought*; since the limits of language and thought are the same an investigation of the former constitutes an investigation of the latter. *This* feature of Wittgenstein's project must be borne in mind throughout, for it is central.

Both Wittgenstein's aim and the way he attempts to attain it cannot be understood properly unless one knows something of the philosophical background to his work. This background consists in developments in logic and philosophy, many of them owing to the writings of Frege and Russell, which had occurred in the decades before the *Tractatus* appeared, and which Wittgenstein had learned from Russell while studying with him at Cambridge. I shall therefore begin by setting out its relevant features.

One matter it is convenient to deal with first concerns the notion of a *proposition* in philosophy, for talk of propositions occurs often in what follows. Leaving aside certain complications, we can say that a proposition is something asserted or proposed for acceptance as true, for example, 'the table is brown', 'this book is about Wittgenstein', 'it is raining'. But propositions are not to be confused with the *sentences* used to express them. A sentence is a grammatically well-formed string of words in any language, written or spoken by someone at a certain time and place. A sentence has only to

prop

obey the grammatical rules of the language to which it belongs in order to be a sentence; it does not have in addition to be 'meaningful'—strings of words like 'green ideas sleep furiously' qualify as sentences despite being nonsensical. A proposition, on the other hand, is *what is asserted* when a sentence (more accurately, a declarative sentence) is meaningfully and non-idly used—and therefore propositions and sentences are quite different things. This difference can best be grasped by noting that *different* sentences, uttered or inscribed by different people at different times and places, may all say the *same* thing—that is, express the same proposition; and that the *same* sentence, used on the same or different occasions by different people, may say *different* things—that is, express different propositions. Here are some examples: the sentences *it is raining*, *il pleut*, *es regnet*, *xia yu*, drawn respectively from English, French, German and Chinese, all express the same proposition, namely that it is raining. This illustrates the first case. Conversely, when *I* say, 'I have a headache', and *you* say, 'I have a headache', two different things are being said (two different propositions expressed) by different uses of the same sentence. This illustrates the second case.

Some philosophers have suggested that we should think of a proposition as the *thought* conveyed by a use of a sentence (or a set of synonymous sentences, whether in the same or different languages). Some, again, have talked of propositions as the *meaning* of sentences, or as the objects which lie before the mind when one knows, believes, remembers, or hopes that something is the case—for example, if Jack believes that Jill loves Jim, then on this view the object of Jack's act of believing is the proposition 'Jill loves Jim'. These proposals are not exclusive of one another; propositions might be all of these things at once. These matters need not detain us now—further and other considerations about the nature of propositions appear later, and for the present this sketch will suffice. What it is important to note now is that in Wittgenstein's theory a proposition is the uttered or written expression of a thought; our interest here, accordingly, does not concern particular sentences of English, German, or Chinese, but the *thoughts expressed* when those sentences are used.

The important background matters relevant to an understanding of the *Tractatus* are the developments in philosophy which resulted, as mentioned above, from work by Frege and Russell. A fruitful way to begin an account of these developments is to look at a problem dealt with by Russell in a celebrated piece of logical analysis.

The problem in question concerns the fact that ordinary language is often philosophically misleading—which is to say, is often misleading as to what we can legitimately think about the world. The problem can be demonstrated in the following way. Consider the two propositions (1) 'the table is brown' and (2) 'the lateness of his arrival was annoying'. The traditional theory of the *structure* of propositions treats them as having two components, namely a subject ('the table', 'the lateness of his arrival') and a predicate ('is brown', 'was annoying'). The subject term refers to something, and the predicate says of that something that it has a certain property or quality. So in (1) the property of brownness is asserted of a given table; in (2) the property of annoyingness is asserted of the lateness of someone's arrival. Now this way of thinking about the structure of propositions, and in particular about the work done by their different parts, leads straight to a difficulty, which a contrast between (1) and (2) brings out. Proposition (1) appears to be unproblematic, because there are indeed tables in the world for the subject term to denote, and we can assert of any suitable one of them that it is brown, which is what we use the predicate term to say. But if we apply the same analysis to (2) then, on the face of it, we seem to be saying that there are *latenesses* in the world, and this should give us pause—for although people and things can indeed arrive or be late, we clearly do not think the world contains things called 'latenesses', at very least in the same sense as we take it to contain tables. The point therefore is that the surface forms of sentences in ordinary language can mask important differences between what is really being said—and therefore thought—in different cases; and this can, and often does, lead to philosophical problems and misunderstandings.

Of course proposition (2) does not present a genuine difficulty, for we can easily rearrange it in such a way that apparent reference to 'latenesses' disappears. We could say 'he arrived annoyingly late', for example. And in order to avoid mistakes in our thinking about the world some such paraphrase is appropriate. This shows that, from a philosophical point of view, it is sometimes necessary to take care with ordinary language in order to keep our thought clear, even to the extent, as in the example just given, of having to recast what we say into a form which avoids misleading implications. This is particularly so when we consider a more serious way in which a proposition can be problematic: which is when, this time, it has what appears to be an unexceptionable subject term, in that like 'the table' but unlike 'the lateness of his arrival' it appears to be a natural and proper expression for occupying the subject place in propositions, in the sense that it appears to denote some existing thing—but which nevertheless does *not* refer to anything. It is to this more difficult case that Russell's famous analysis applies.

Consider the proposition 'the present King of France is wise'. This is perfectly meaningful, and because it is so it seems natural to ask whether it is true or false. And to this there seems an equally natural answer. There is no King of France at present; the subject term fails to refer to anything. Therefore it seems that the proposition should be considered false. But there is a problem here, concerning how to demonstrate *why* it is false. This is because if in normal circumstances we say of something (call it 'x') that x is wise, the proposition 'x is wise' will be true if x *is* wise, and false if x is *not* wise. But what if there is no x? How can we say of something that does not exist that it either is or is not wise?

Initially Russell accepted a solution to this puzzle which had been proposed by the nineteenth-century philosopher Alexius Meinong. This solution was to say that every expression with a referring or denoting function in a sentence *does* denote something, either an actually existing item, as with the table in 'the table is brown', or a 'subsisting' item, where by 'subsistence' is meant non-actual existence—a kind of real but half or 'courtesy' existence. On this view, the universe contains everything that can be thought or talked about, including the present King of France; but only some of what the universe contains is *actually* existent. Accordingly the descriptive phrase 'the present King of France' does indeed denote, and what it denotes is a subsistent—that is a real but non-actual—King of France.

Meinong's view is not as extravagant as it seems, for it is based on a consideration which is both right and important. This is that thought is *intentional*, that is, is directed towards or focused upon an object, where what is meant by an 'object' is whatever is mentioned when one answers the question 'what are you thinking about?' Suppose someone asks me this question when I am thinking about my table, and I therefore reply 'the table'. The table is the object 'intended' by my thought: it is what my thought is *about*. Similarly, if I am thinking about a dryad, the object or 'intention' of my thought is a dryad. In the first case what I am thinking about—the table—actually exists in the world; in the second case, the object of my thought has merely intentional existence, that is, exists only as an object or intention of a thought. In either case the object intended by the thought is whatever the thought is about or is directed towards. So far, there is no difficulty. But Meinong went further by arguing that since a dryad can be intended by your thoughts as well as mine, her existence as an object of thought is in an important way independent of either of our acts of thinking about her, and that therefore she has a real existence even although she is not *actual* in the sense of being encounterable in the world in the same way as the table. In Meinong's terminology, in short, the dryad subsists.

Russell could not rest content with this theory for long. The idea of subsisting entities is obviously difficult to swallow, and Russell said of it that it soon came to offend his 'vivid sense of reality'. One quick way of showing why is to note that if this theory were right, each of us would have infinite numbers of subsistent but non-actual brothers and sisters; they, along with all the infinities of other subsistent entities, together with all the actually existing ones, would make for an overcrowded universe indeed. Accordingly Russell set about finding an analysis of propositions like 'the present King of France is wise' which would explain their meaningfulness and their

19

possession of truth or falsity without having to invoke a notion of subsistence. He did so by arguing that names and descriptive phrases occupying *grammatical* subject place in sentences are not genuine referring expressions at all, and that therefore sentences which contain them in grammatical subject place are misleading as to the proper *logical* form of the propositions they express. Thus 'the present King of France is wise' should correctly be seen as shorthand for a conjunction of three propositions asserting (1) that there is a King of France, (2) that there is only one King of France (this takes care of the definite article, 'the', which implies uniqueness), and (3) that whatever is King of France is wise. Since (1) is false, the original proposition is false. Proper names like 'Henry' are to be treated in the same way, for they can be viewed as disguised descriptions; if we say 'Henry is wise' we are asserting (1) there is something which is Henry, (2) there is, in the relevant context, only one such thing, and (3) that thing is wise. If all of (1)–(3) are true, 'Henry is wise' is true; if either (1) or (3) is false, 'Henry is wise' is false. What is happening here is that we are *analysing* the given propositions into their *logical form*, represented by the conjunction of (1)–(3) in each case; and this reveals what we are really saying (and therefore thinking) in a quite perspicuous way—a way which, moreover, involves no appeal to subsistent entities and the like.

Russell's 'Theory of Descriptions', as the foregoing analysis is called, illustrates something centrally important for an understanding of Wittgenstein's *Tractatus*, namely what is meant by talk of the *logical structure* or *logical form* which underlies ordinary language, investigating which promises to tell us much of philosophical significance about the nature of language and thought themselves. And it is, as noted above, just such an investigation which constitutes the chief task of the *Tractatus*. Wittgenstein much admired Russell's 'Theory of Descriptions', which in his early period he took to be a paradigm of how philosophical problems should be dealt with. He comments in the *Tractatus*: 'All philosophy is a "critique of language" . . . It was Russell who performed the service of showing that the apparent logical form of a proposition need not be its real one' (T 4.0031).

The concept of logical form involves more than has so far appeared, however, in particular concerning the nature of the *logic* in terms of which that underlying form is to be described. This too is important—indeed, essential—for an understanding of the *Tractatus*, and accordingly something must be said about it.

When Russell gave an analysis of the sentence 'the present King of France is wise' to reveal its logical form, he did not do so by using the three English sentences numbered (1)–(3) above, for the reason that the risk of misleadingness which attaches to the original sentence might well reappear in the analysis represented by (1)–(3), since (1)–(3) are themselves sentences of ordinary language. Instead he used the language of logic, which he regarded as 'the perfect language' because of its precision and clarity. The attraction is obvious; if one can translate or at least paraphrase sentences of ordinary language into a wholly perspicuous formal language which reveals exactly what is being said without risk of misunderstanding, then one can lay bare to one's view the structure of legitimate thought about the world. Wittgenstein later described this as uncovering the 'hidden essence' of thought. And this project becomes yet more attractive when one realizes that there are certain other features of the 'perfect language' which promise to help us understand the nature of thought. One such, apart from the notion of 'logical form' already encountered, is that of 'truth-functionality'. To explain this and other notions requires a brief account of logic itself, as follows. (There are some simple technicalities in the next few pages; the symbols used will not reappear elsewhere in what follows, although the ideas associated with them will—which is why it is important that they be explained.)

Modern treatments of logic begin with Gottlob Frege, whose major works were written in the closing decades of the nineteenth century. Until Frege, logic had in essentials retained the character given to it by Aristotle, who made the first systematic investigation of the subject two and a half millennia ago. Logic was indeed regarded as a completed science well into the nineteenth century. Frege's discoveries and innovations were revolutionary, rendering logic at once

21

simpler, more powerful, and more extensive than traditional logic. In important part this was because he invented a symbolic language, based on arithmetic, which enabled him to explore the subject with greater facility and depth than had hitherto been possible. He called his symbolic language a 'concept script', and used it to construct a set of new and fundamental logical notions which are now central to the subject. Wittgenstein's argument in the *Tractatus* in part turns on these notions, and develops certain of them in original ways. In order to explain them I shall not use Frege's 'concept script' but a common variant of the symbolism invented by Russell and his collaborator A. N. Whitehead in *Principia Mathematica* (1910–12). This symbolism has so many advantages over Frege's pioneering attempts that it now constitutes the basis of standard logical notations.

The primary concern in logic is to identify and classify valid forms of inference. The notions of 'validity', 'form', and 'inference' are the key ones. They can be explained in the following way. Consider these two arguments: (1) 'Either Tom broke the clock or Harry did. Harry did not break the clock. Therefore Tom did.' (2) 'Either it rained on Tuesday or on Wednesday. But on Wednesday there was no rain. Therefore it rained on Tuesday.' Each of these arguments has two premisses from which a conclusion, introduced by 'therefore', is drawn. The premisses constitute the grounds for the conclusion. To draw a conclusion from premisses is to *infer* it from them. If a conclusion can be inferred validly from its premisses, then we say that the premisses *entail* the conclusion or that the conclusion *follows from* the premisses.

The briefest inspection shows that (1) and (2) have the same structure or form; they each say 'either p or q; not q; therefore p'. What the logician is interested in is the question whether, leaving aside particularities of clocks or the weather, arguments of this *form* are such that their conclusions *always* follow from their premisses. More precisely, his interest is to identify those forms of argument which are such that *if* their premisses are true, their conclusions are guaranteed to be true also.

It is important to note that the logician's only interest

concerns an argument's form, not the truth or falsity of its premisses and conclusion. When it happens that the premisses of a given valid argument are in fact true, then such an argument is said to be not just valid but *sound*, which is a further matter. The distinction between validity and soundness is a significant one, for many arguments can be valid with respect to their form ('formally valid') without being sound, that is, without guaranteeing the truth of their conclusions, as in this case: (3) 'either the moon is not made of green cheese or it orbits the earth. But the moon does not orbit the earth. Therefore it is not made of green cheese.' This argument is valid, but unsound, for its second premiss is false. There are many other ways in which arguments can be valid but unsound. This is why validity is explained in terms of an important 'if': validity is the property an argument has when its *form* is such that *IF* the premisses are true, the truth of the conclusion is guaranteed.

Given that it is validity and not soundness which constitutes the logician's primary interest, it is unnecessary to take account of particular considerations about clocks, the weather, the moon, or any other matter of fact, but only the structure or form of arguments. This permits a useful simplification; one can use symbols to stand for propositions, as was done above in illustrating the form shared by (1) and (2), (and also (3)). The letters 'p', 'q', and their successors in the alphabet are standardly employed for this purpose. The letters so used are of course not themselves propositions; they are *formulae* which 'stand for' propositions in the literal sense that they occupy the places in the argument where the proposition would occur if we were to write out in full the sentences which express them.

The next step is to look at the way propositions can be combined together to make more complex ones. In (1) the first premiss, 'either Tom broke the clock or Harry did', is a complex proposition made up of two simple propositions, 'Tom broke the clock' and 'Harry broke the clock', connected by 'or'. The form is 'p or q'. The compound formula 'p or q' is of course a *single* formula; it differs from the uncompounded or 'atomic' formulae, namely 'p' taken by itself and 'q' taken by itself, only in being compound. Compound formulae can themselves be elements of larger compounds. Suppose we have 'p or q' and another compound formula 'r or s'. Then we can combine them with 'or' to yield the single formula '(p or q) or (r or s)', using the brackets in an intuitive way to keep everything clear. This process of building up more and more complex formulae can go on indefinitely.

Apart from 'or' there are other connectives of great importance, namely 'and' and 'if . . . then . . .'. These also join atomic formulae together to make compound formulae. We can write such formulae 'p and q', 'if p then q' respectively. To simplify matters further, logicians use signs to stand for 'or', 'and', and 'if . . . then . . .' thus: the sign 'v' serves for 'or' (it is drawn from the Latin *vel*, 'or'); the sign '&' serves for 'and'; and the arrow '→' serves for 'if . . . then . . .'. So we write 'pvq', 'p&q', 'p→q' respectively.

How these connectives work is the really important issue, both for an understanding of logic and an appreciation of Wittgenstein's early philosophy. Indeed, the account now to be given of these connectives is drawn from a treatment of them suggested by Wittgenstein in the *Tractatus*. The central idea is that the truth or falsity (for short, the 'truth-value') of a compound proposition depends wholly upon the truth-values of its constituent atomic propositions. For example, the truth-value of a proposition symbolized as 'p&q' depends upon the truth-values of 'p' and of 'q' taken separately. This is expressed by saying that compound propositions are *truth-functions* of their component atomic propositions. A simple table illustrates what is meant. Under the atomic formulae 'p' and 'q' we write all the possible combinations of truth-values which they can have between them, like this:

p	q
T	T
T	F
F	T
F	F

Here 'T' stands for 'true' and 'F' for 'false'. Next we show under what conditions the compound formula 'p&q' is true. What this asserts is that *both* 'p' and 'q' are true. So we add a column under the heading 'p&q' to show that the only case in which 'p&q' is true is when each of 'p' and 'q' is independently true:

p	q	p&q
T	T	T
T	F	F
F	T	F
F	F	F

This table—called a 'truth-table'—is in effect a picture of how '&' works. The same can be done for the other connectives. For example, understanding 'pvq' to mean 'either p or q or both', we write the truth table as follows:

p	q	pvq
T	T	T
T	F	T
F	T	T
F	F	F

This shows that 'pvq' is true if at least one of 'p' or 'q' is true, and false only if both 'p' and 'q' are false, just as we would expect. The important point is that the truth-value of the compound formulae 'p&q', 'pvq' is determined by—that is, is a *function* of—the truth-values of their constituent atomic formulae and the way these are combined. Accordingly the connectives '&', 'v', '→' are called *truth-functional connectives*, or, more generally 'truth-functors'.

There is another important logical word, namely 'not', which, although not a connective (it does not join together propositions or the formulae which symbolize them), is nevertheless a truth-functor. Logicians use the sign ' – ' to serve for 'not', and write ' – p' for 'not p'. The way ' – ' works is described by its simple truth-table:

p	$-$p
T	F
F	T

When 'p' is true, ' $-$ p' is false; when 'p' is false, ' $-$ p' is true. It follows that if a compound formula, say 'pvq', is true, then its negation, written ' $-$ (pvq)', is false; and vice versa. Note how the brackets are used to show that the negation sign applies to the whole formula 'pvq'; if we were to write ' $-$ pvq' we would be saying something quite different, namely 'not p, or q'.

The letters and truth-functors are the elements of a language which, together with certain rules of inference taken as primitive or axiomatic, constitute what is called the *'propositional calculus'*. It allows logicians to explore the logical relations between whole propositions in a completely systematic way. The addition of a few more symbols and rules enables logicians to get *inside* propositions, as it were, in order to examine the nature of valid inference when the internal structure of propositions matters. For example, a proposition like 'the table is brown', which would be represented by, say, 'p' if a logician were concerned only to investigate its relations to other whole propositions, can be symbolized for these more detailed purposes as 'x is F', or, more succinctly, 'Fx', where 'x' is an individual variable (stands for individual things) and 'F' is a predicate letter standing in this case for ' $-\!\!-\!\!-$ is brown'. Then we get formulae like 'Fx v Gx', pronounced 'x is F or x is G'. Note that the truth-functor 'v' continues to function in accordance with its truth-table as demonstrated above.

A final step is to introduce ways of symbolizing propositions like 'all humans are mortal' and 'some humans are tall'. These contain *quantifier* expressions, 'all' and 'some', indicating how many things have a certain property—in this case, how many humans are mortal or tall. Logicians write '(x)' to symbolize 'all x' or 'every x'; thus 'all humans are mortal' is in symbolic form '(x)(Hx $\rightarrow$ Mx)', pronounced 'for all x, if x is human then x is mortal'. The quantifier 'some' can most usefully be expressed as 'at least one', and logicians write '($\exists$ x)' to symbolize 'there is at least one x' or more briefly 'there is an x'. Thus 'some humans are tall' is symbolized '$(\exists x)(Hx \ \& \ Tx)$', pronounced 'there is an x such that x is human and x is tall'. When these notions are added to the propositional calculus the resulting language is called the *predicate calculus*; it is a simple but extremely powerful language which equips logicians to explore the forms of valid inference, and which provides philosophers with a tool for investigating the structure of language and thought.

This language—the language of the predicate calculus—is what Russell called 'the perfect language'. In the case of 'the present King of France is wise' Russell used it to give the *full analysis* of that problematic sentence—that is, the complete description of its logical form. The analysis is:

$$(\exists x)((Kx \ \& \ (y)(Ky \rightarrow y = x)) \ \& \ Wx)$$

where 'K' stands for 'King of France' and 'W' for 'wise'. The whole formula is pronounced 'there is something, call it x, such that x is King of France; and for anything else, call it y, if y is King of France then y and x are identical (this shows that there is only *one* King of France); and x is wise'. This may look somewhat complicated, but is not so; the chief point is that there is nothing misleading about the logical formula into which 'the present King of France is wise' has been analysed, and hence, once the eye is accustomed to symbolism, all is perspicuous—we know exactly what is being said and hence thought, for the analysis brings its logical structure explicitly into view. Recall Wittgenstein's aim: it is to show that the problems of philosophy will be solved once we grasp how our language works. The workings of language depend upon its underlying logical structure; therefore to solve the problems of philosophy we must, says Wittgenstein, make clear to ourselves the nature of that underlying logical structure. *This* shows the importance of logic in Wittgenstein's *Tractatus*.

A central notion in the foregoing account of logic is *truth-functionality*, explained, as we have seen, in terms of the truth-tables showing how the truth-values of compound formulae depend upon the truth-values of their constituent atomic formulae and the way they are combined. One more example will help to fix this idea clearly. Consider the complex formula

27

'(pvq) & (rvs)'. The truth-value of this formula depends upon that of 'pvq' and of 'rvs' taken independently; and the truth-values of these two formulae, in *their* turn, depend upon the truth-values of their parts—in the case of 'pvq' on the truth-values of 'p' and of 'q' taken independently, and in the case of 'rvs' on the truth-values of 'r' and 's' taken independently. So the whole complex formula '(pvq) & (rvs)' has a truth-value which in the end depends on that of each of the simple or atomic formulae 'p', 'q', 'r', 's', which are its ultimate constituents or 'atoms'; it is a truth-function of those atoms and the way they are put together by means of the connectives 'v' and '&'. This idea plays a crucial role in the *Tractatus*.

2 *The argument of the* Tractatus

Armed with the foregoing sketch of background ideas we can now turn to Wittgenstein's *Tractatus* itself. A preliminary point to note concerns how the *Tractatus* is structured. It was Wittgenstein's method, one which he employed throughout his life, to write down his ideas in the form of theses and remarks upon these theses, subsequently arranging them into an appropriate overall order. In the *Tractatus* Wittgenstein expresses his view in the form of seven theses, and the bulk of the book consists in comments upon and expansions of each of the first six, together with subordinate comments upon and expansions of these higher-order remarks themselves. To keep the structure of the argument clearly in view Wittgenstein uses a system of decimal numbering. The system is one which anyone familiar with business or official reports can quickly grasp; chief points are marked with whole numbers (1, 2, etc.), comments subordinate to these with a single decimal (1.1, 2.1, etc.), points subordinate to these latter with two decimals (1.11, 2.11, etc.), and so on in the standard way. The *Tractatus* is rather elaborate structurally, yielding remark-numbers with as many as five decimals, for example 2.02331; but the principle of the arrangement is straightforward, as described. References to the *Tractatus* are always effected simply by quoting the relevant remark number.

A second point to note is that although the *Tractatus* is a short book, the range of topics it covers is very wide. In the course of its main argument concerning language, the world, and the relation between them, the *Tractatus* also deals with the following: the nature of logic and logical form; probability; the concept of number; induction and causality; the purpose of philosophy; solipsism; and questions about ethics, religion, and life. The treatment accorded most of these topics is very brief, and in consequence the *Tractatus*'s comments upon them seem aphoristic and obscure. But Wittgenstein's views on these matters are either consequences or corollaries of his main argument, to which all these topics are intimately linked, and accordingly a grasp of that argument makes his meaning in these respects fairly clear, as we shall see when we consider some of them.

I shall begin by setting out the main argument of the *Tractatus* in summary form, afterwards returning to explain each of its main themes in more detail.

Both language and the world, Wittgenstein says, have a structure. Language consists in propositions, and these are compounds made up of what he calls 'elementary' propositions, which in turn are combinations of names. Names are the ultimate constituents of language. Correspondingly, the world consists in the totality of facts, and facts are compounded out of 'states of affairs', which in turn are compounded out of objects. Each level of structure in language matches a level of structure in the world. The objects, which are the ultimate constituents of the world, are denoted by the ultimate constituents of language, the names; names combine to form elementary propositions, which correspond to states of affairs; and each of these further combine to form, respectively, propositions and the facts which, in a sense to be explained, those propositions 'picture'. Here, in a crude preliminary form, is a representation of the two parallel structures:

Language		World
	⟷	
│		│
propositions	⟷	facts
│		│
elementary propositions	⟷	states of affairs
│		│
names	⟷	objects

This representation is crude because it does not show how the vertical and horizontal relationships between the two sets of levels work; but it is a useful preliminary sketch.

The correspondence between elementary propositions and states of affairs is constituted by the fact that the names out of which elementary propositions are built denote the objects out of which their correspondent states of affairs are built; the *arrangement* of the names logically mirrors or pictures the arrangement of the objects in states of affairs. It is in virtue of this picturing relation that the propositions compounded out of elementary propositions have sense. This is the 'picture theory of meaning' which lies at the heart of the *Tractatus*, constituting the explanation of how language and the world are connected, and therefore of how meaning attaches to what we say when we use language correctly. Much more will be said of this below.

The elementary propositions are logically independent of each other. Because this is so, we need to say which of them are true and which false in order to give a complete account of reality. This is equivalent to saying that reality consists of all possible states of affairs, whether existing or non-existing. In other words, how everything actually *is* in reality depends upon what is and what is not the case; and that is why we need to know which elementary propositions are true and which false, for only then can we specify how things actually stand in reality.

Propositions are formed out of elementary propositions by the truth-functional connectives (more exactly, by a single truth-functional connective in terms of which all the others can be defined). They are therefore *truth-functions* of elementary propositions. Because they depend for their own truth-value on the truth-values of the elementary propositions which constitute them, propositions will be true or false according to the distribution of the truth-values among the elementary propositions. But there are two important cases where this is not so: one in which a proposition is *true no matter what its constituents' truth-values*, and the other in which a proposition is *false no matter what its constituents' truth-values*. In the first case the proposition is a *tautology*, always true; in the second it is a *contradiction*, always false. The true propositions of logic are tautologies, and the true propositions of mathematics may be considered so too. Neither logical nor mathematical propositions say anything about the world, however, because in virtue of their always being true they are consistent with *any* way the world could happen to be (with the existence or non-existence of *any* state of affairs).

When a sign or string of signs fails to express a proposition it is nonsense. It is not that such a sign or string of signs says something *false*; it is that it says *nothing at all*, for it fails to picture anything in the world and hence has no connection with the world. Wittgenstein includes 'most of the propositions of philosophy' in this class. Because this is so he says at the end of the *Tractatus*: 'My propositions serve as elucidations in the following way: anyone who understands me eventually recognizes them as nonsensical, when he has used them—as steps—to climb up beyond them. (He must, so to speak, throw away the ladder after he has climbed up it.)' (T6.54; the image of the discardable ladder comes from Schopenhauer.) The limits of what can significantly be said— and therefore thought—thus turn out to be imposed by the structure of both language and the world, and by the way they connect with each other through the 'picturing' relation. Only when such a connection obtains do our signs (the expressions of our language) have sense. And because the content of ethics, religion, and the 'problems of life' lie *outside* the world— outside the realm of facts and their constituent states of affairs—nothing can be *said* about them. To try to say anything about them is, given the way language works, to fall into nonsense. This does not, as mentioned, mean that ethics and the rest are themselves nonsense. It is only the attempt to talk about them which is so. In Wittgenstein's view matters of ethical and religious significance *show* themselves; they cannot be *stated*. Wittgenstein considered this to be a crucially important point, and was careful to indicate that the ultimate aim of the *Tractatus* is indeed to reveal, via the argument about language (thought) and the manner of its connection with the world, just what the status of ethical and religious values is.

This summary of the *Tractatus*'s argument is very compressed. Making it clearer requires going through its main points step by step, adding some of the detail which explains Wittgenstein's intentions more fully. The first step is to grasp more clearly Wittgenstein's views about each of the levels of structure in language and the world; the second step is to understand his 'picture theory' of how language and world are linked.

What Wittgenstein says about the structure of language and the world is very abstract. He does not, when talking of how the world is, give examples of facts, states of affairs, and objects; nor does he give examples, in describing the structure of language, of propositions, elementary propositions, and names. This is deliberate. He relies on an undefined and perhaps intuitive grasp of what 'propositions' and 'facts' are, and then specifies their respective finer structures in terms of what these structures *must* be like in order for it to be possible that language should (as it manifestly does) succeed in connecting with the world. In Wittgenstein's view it is the task of an empirical enquiry—specifically, psychology—to determine the practical question of how we link language to the world in our experience and activity, just as it is the task of natural science to describe the structure and properties of physical things. The task in philosophy, in Wittgenstein's view, is by contrast the wholly conceptual one of identifying the logical conditions which must obtain for there to be a link between world and language.

A comparison with Russell's views is informative here. Working from some of the same basic ideas (because of his early collaboration with Wittgenstein) but with empirical considerations expressly in view, Russell likewise argues that the relation between language and world depends upon the fact that the simplest elements of each are directly linked. But in Russell's theory the mechanism is somewhat different. The link between language and the world is, for Russell as for Wittgenstein, the relation of denotation. But for Russell the 'atoms' of language are the demonstrative pronouns 'this' and 'that', and the atoms of the world are 'sense-data', that is, bits of information (for example, colour-patches, sensations of touch, sounds) gathered by our five senses. The link is forged by the use we make of the demonstrative pronouns to refer directly to sense-data. So in Russell's view language connects with the world because at this most basic level we 'name', by means of the demonstratives, the items of sensory information which constitute our immediate experiential contact with the world. It is interesting to observe that in his notebooks Wittgenstein shows that he began by thinking much along the same lines as Russell. Nevertheless he decided to restrict attention to the *logical* basis of the issues, and therefore did not investigate their 'psychological' aspects as Russell had done. It is this which gives the *Tractatus* its highly abstract character.

Wittgenstein's account of the world's structure occurs at the beginning of the *Tractatus*. It is useful to look at the way he sets out his principal theses on this head before embarking on a discussion of them. From the sketch given above it will be remembered that the chief elements of that structure are *facts*, which are composed of *states of affairs*, which are in turn composed of *objects*. Wittgenstein states this as follows:

1   The world is all that is the case.
1.1   The world is the totality of facts, not of things.
2   What is the case—a fact—is the existence of states of affairs.
2.01   A state of affairs (a state of things) is a combination of objects (things).
2.02   Objects are simple.

This is the basic structure. After setting it out Wittgenstein adds some remarks on the *nature* of the relation between the levels:

2.0271 Objects are what is unalterable and subsistent; their configuration is what is changing and unstable.
2.032   The determinate way in which objects are connected in states of affairs is the structure of the state of affairs.
2.034   The structure of a fact consists of the structure of states of affairs.
2.04   The totality of existing states of affairs is the world.

2.05   The totality of existing states of affairs also determines which states of affairs do not exist.

2.06   The existence and non-existence of states of affairs is reality.

Each of these theses carries a heavy load of significance and requires explanation. The first (thesis 1) states that the world is everything that *is*. Since, as we shall see, Wittgenstein goes on to argue that the world is represented by propositions, and that propositions are true or false according to whether they represent or fail to represent what is the case, it follows that the world is everything that is represented by the totality of true propositions. This conception is fundamental to Wittgenstein's claims about what can legitimately be said, and what therefore cannot be said but only shown. Coming to a conclusion on these matters is the *Tractatus*'s aim; Wittgenstein's central concerns are therefore present from the outset.

The second and subsequent theses concern the world's structure itself. Thesis 1.1 says that the world is not to be identified with the sum of *things* which exist in it—it is not a collection of objects like, say, stones, teacups, subatomic particles, or whatever empirical science says 'objects' are—but rather is the totality of *facts*. Examples of 'facts' might roughly be that I am writing these words at a certain time and place, that Everest is the highest mountain on this planet, that our solar system is located in a spiral galaxy, and so on. Wittgenstein himself does not give such examples, but proceeds directly to an abstract specification of facts as 'the existence of states of affairs'. The notion of 'states of affairs' is difficult to explain other than intuitively. For the sake merely of illustration, we might say that my sitting at a desk holding a pen, my doing so in Oxford in the springtime, and so on, are among the states of affairs—the 'ways things are', the situations that exist—which together constitute the fact that I am writing these words at a certain time and place. Again, Wittgenstein expressly avoids giving such examples. He defines a state of affairs in an austerely abstract fashion as *a combination of objects*, meaning by this that a state of affairs is such that one can break it down ('analyse' it) into component parts; the component parts, together with their arrangements, are the ultimate building blocks of the state of affairs. These building blocks are *objects*, and objects are 'simple' in the sense of being uncompounded, that is, having no structure. They therefore cannot be broken down or analysed into something more fundamental than themselves. They constitute the primitive elements out of which the world is constituted. Moreover, it is *essential* to objects, Wittgenstein says, that they be possible constituents of states of affairs; the thought of an object which could exist outside any possible combination of objects (any state of affairs) is an empty thought. Since this is so, if we had a complete inventory of all the objects there are, we would know all the states of affairs there could possibly be, because knowing anything about a given object involves knowing what combinations it is its essential nature to belong to— and this is just to know what states of affairs are possible.

The fact that they are 'simple' means that objects do not change. It is their combinations and arrangements which do so. But when objects are in combination, thus constituting a state of affairs, there is nothing indeterminate about their arrangement: each such combination has a *definite* character. This determinateness of arrangement is the *structure* of a state of affairs. The structure of facts, likewise, is determined by the structure of the states of affairs constituting them. Accordingly a complete analysis of a fact has as its termination a specification of a determinate combination of objects. And this means that each fact has only one correct analysis, because each fact ultimately consists in a particular and definite combination of the members of a particular and definite set of objects.

The last two theses noted above—2.05 and 2.06—add a further important consideration. It is that the states of affairs which exist settle which states of affairs do *not* exist. For example, matters are such that I am holding a pen, and this excludes the state of affairs consisting in my being empty-handed. Since in this way *how things are* determines *how they are not*, reality as a whole is the totality of existing states of affairs together with everything their existence excludes as non-existent.

Wittgenstein's account of the world's structure is almost as brief as it is abstract; it occupies the first four pages of the *Tractatus* only. Immediately after stating it he turns his attention to the 'picture' theory and language. But an understanding of these latter turns crucially on the account he gives of the world's structure, which is why the *Tractatus* begins with it. When it comes to the structure of *language*, as we shall now see, Wittgenstein relies on the above account to explain the nature and role of the different levels of language themselves.

It is useful, as before, to begin by setting out Wittgenstein's main theses concerning the '*propositions–elementary propositions–names*' structure of language. As one reads through them one should keep in mind two matters: first, the foregoing account of the world's structure, and secondly, the thesis—to be explained more fully below—that language connects with the world by means of a 'picturing' relation. It is necessary to anticipate one point about the picture theory at this juncture, however: it is that, for Wittgenstein, when one *thinks* about something in the world—a fact—one's thought is a *logical picture* of that fact, and that since propositions are *expressions of thoughts*, propositions are therefore themselves pictures of facts. This comes out clearly in the theses on language structure. The theses are these:

3.   A logical picture of facts is a thought.
3.1   In a proposition a thought finds an expression that can be perceived by the senses.
3.2   In a proposition a thought can be expressed in such a way that the elements of the propositional sign correspond to the objects of the thought.
3.201   I call such elements 'simple signs', and such a proposition 'completely analysed'.
3.25   A proposition has one and only one complete analysis.
3.203   A name means an object. The object is its meaning.
3.22   In a proposition a name is a representative of an object.

3.26   A name cannot be dissected further by means of a definition: it is a primitive sign.

Remark 3.25 parallels the thesis, discussed above, that each fact has a particular and definite structure, so that an analysis of that fact—which is the same thing as an analysis of the proposition corresponding to it—will result in a description of a particular and definite combination of objects. The objects are denoted by the names, the 'simple signs' which are the 'elements' (the ultimate building blocks) of propositions; this is made clear by the last three remarks above. Wittgenstein goes on:

4.001   The totality of propositions is language.
4.11   The totality of true propositions is the whole of natural science.

These two theses are direct corollaries of what Wittgenstein says about the respective structures of language and the world and the way they connect through the picturing relation. In them lies the substance of his claim that only *factual* discourse is possible: he puts the same point more explicitly later by saying 'nothing . . . can be said [except] the propositions of natural science' (T 6.53). And from this it immediately follows that we cannot say anything about what falls outside the domain of facts as described by science, namely, matters of *value*, that is, ethics and religion. The two theses just quoted —4.001 and 4.11—are therefore central; it is typical of the *Tractatus*'s elaborately arranged and compressed argument that they appear before the whole of that argument has been given. Nor do they appear together, as I have given them here; their decimal numbers show that they are separated by discussion of several important subsidiary issues, including these:

4.01   A proposition is a picture of reality.
4.022   A proposition *shows* its sense.
        A proposition *shows* how things stand *if* it is true. And it *says* that they do so stand.
4.023   A proposition must restrict reality to two alternatives: yes or no.

In order to do that, it must describe reality completely.

The picture theory of the language-world relationship is inseparable from Wittgenstein's account of propositions. In 4.01 the claim that propositions are pictures is expressly made. We shall shortly investigate how the picturing relation works. It is essential for Wittgenstein's conception of propositions as pictures of reality that propositions should be *determinate* in truth-value; they are true or they are false, and which they are depends on whether they fit the facts or fail to do so. There is no question of a partial or fuzzy correspondence between propositions and facts: the only alternatives are 'yes' and 'no'—either a proposition is a picture of a fact, or it is not. And this has to be the case, Wittgenstein says, because—once more—of the *structure* of propositions, namely that propositions are truth-functions of elementary propositions, which are themselves structures of names:

5   A proposition is a truth-function of elementary propositions.

4.21   The simplest kind of propositions, an elementary proposition, asserts the existence of a state of affairs.

4.25   If an elementary proposition is true, the state of affairs exists; if an elementary proposition is false, the state of affairs does not exist.

4.22   An elementary proposition consists of names. It is a nexus, a concatenation of names.

4.24   Names are the simple symbols.

Setting all these theses alongside those about the world makes Wittgenstein's conception of both quite clear. From the basis of the parallel structures upwards, the relations between them are as follows: names denote objects, and like objects they are simple and unanalysable; elementary propositions are 'concatenations of names' and they assert the existence of states of affairs, which are concatenations of objects; and propositions—the perceptible expressions of thoughts (perceptible because one can read or hear the 'propositional signs' used to express them)—are truth-functions of elementary propositions. This account is wholly formal: Wittgenstein does not, as noted, give examples of names and elementary propositions or of what they correspond to in the world; his account is devoted solely to saying that it is necessary, in order for there to *be* a language-world link, that the structures of both *must* be like this, whatever as a matter of fact plays the role of the names, objects, and the rest, as specified in that account.

The austerely formal nature of the account, together with the paucity of concrete examples, might seem puzzling until one recalls that Wittgenstein's interest lies solely in the *logical* character which world and language must possess in order for connections between them to be possible. Think of the logician's interest in discovering the nature of valid argument forms, as described in the preceding section: it is unnecessary to bother with particular propositions—expressed by sentences of one or another natural language—concerned with particular things like clocks, the moon, or anything else, but only with the *form* of the argument, using a symbolism ('p', 'q', '&', 'v', and so on) to make that form explicit. This is what Wittgenstein is doing in the *Tractatus*. It is enough for his purposes to say something like this: the proposition 'p&q' is a truth-function of the elementary propositions 'p' and 'q'; 'p' is a concatenation of names 'w' and 'x', and 'q' is a concatenation of names 'y' and 'z'; and each of these levels of structure mirrors a concomitant level of structure in the world. (Wittgenstein does not put matters quite like this in the *Tractatus*, but it serves as an illustration; see T 4.24.) It is in this way that Wittgenstein's account is a purely *formal* or *structural* one. And it explains why he thought, unlike Russell, that 'psychological' questions—questions about what objects are, and how we come to denote them by the names which are the primitive elements of language—were no part of his enterprise.

Now that the parallel language-world structures have been described it is possible to set out the crucial matter of the 'picturing' relation in which Wittgenstein says their connection with each other consists. This is the key to the argument so far, and this time Wittgenstein provides plenty of examples to show what he means.

The idea of the picture theory was suggested to Wittgenstein, as he reports in his *Notebooks*, by reading a newspaper description of how toy motor cars and dolls were used in a Paris court-room to depict the facts of something then relatively new in the world, a motor-accident. The models pictured reality by being arranged in a way exactly corresponding to the disposition of the real people and vehicles at the time of the accident. This raises a question: what is it for something to be a picture of something else? What is it about the miniature street-scene in the Paris court-room which makes it a *picture* of reality? Wittgenstein begins by offering an answer to this question.

2.12   A picture is a model of reality.

2.131   In a picture the elements of the picture are the representatives of objects.

2.14   What constitutes a picture is that its elements are related to one another in a determinate way.

2.15   The fact that the elements of a picture are related to one another in a determinate way represents that things are related to one another in the same way.

So much is obvious. Wittgenstein then says that the possibility that things in reality can be represented by pictures—that is, can have their arrangement displayed by the arrangement of a picture's elements—rests on the fact that pictures have something in common with the reality they depict; and what they have in common is of course their *structure*. Take a straightforward case: suppose you are painting a still life of a hat standing to the left of a pair of boots on a chair. If your painting is to depict that collection of objects just as it is, its structure must accord with that of the objects' arrangement; the hat must stand to the left of the boots in the picture. This shared structure Wittgenstein calls *pictorial form*:

2.151   Pictorial form is the possibility that things are related to one another in the same way as the elements of a picture.

2.161   There must be something identical in a picture and what it depicts, to enable one to be a picture of the other at all.

2.17   What a picture must have in common with reality in order to be able to depict it—correctly or incorrectly—in the way that it does, is pictorial form.

It is pictorial form, therefore, understood as the possibility of identity of structure between a picture and what it depicts, which makes the picturing relationship possible. But there is a further point: the structure shared between picture and reality is a structure of elements—the elements of the picture, and the elements of the depicted reality. The *link* between a particular picture and reality is a link between their respective elements:

2.1514 The pictorial relationship consists of the correlations of the picture's elements with things.

2.1515 These correlations are, as it were, the feelers of the picture's elements, with which the picture touches reality.

2.1511 *That* is how a picture is attached to reality; it reaches right out to it.

2.1512 It is laid against reality like a ruler.

All these theses are the answer to the question about what constitutes a picture. The transition to the crucial thesis that *propositions* are pictures, in just this sense, is effected by Wittgenstein in two brief steps. The first consists in his stating that every picture is a *logical* picture (T 2.182). What this means can be put as follows. Pictures are not all of the same kind—not all pictures are, say, spatial ones; if a monotone picture depicts things as coloured, it cannot use colour to do so; and so on—but *every* picture has pictorial form, that is, the essential possibility of possessing a community of structure with what it depicts, and only if something satisfies this minimum requirement can it *be* a picture. The point here therefore concerns the *logical* condition for a picture to be a picture. The condition is a logical one because it turns solely on considerations about the form or structure which, when the picturing relation obtains, must of necessity be shared by the picture and what it depicts so that the picturing relation can obtain between them. Therefore, Wittgenstein says, pictorial form *is* logical form (T 2.181 and 2.182 again). And this means that anything possessing a logical form is a picture.

Wittgenstein's second step concerns truth and falsity. He says: 'A picture agrees with reality or fails to agree; it is correct or incorrect, true or false' (T 2.21). The point is intended to be intuitive. If a picture successfully shows how things are in reality, it 'agrees' with that reality, and we therefore say that it is a correct depiction. Where the picture in question is a thought or proposition, we call its agreement with reality 'truth' and the converse 'falsity'. The division between 'agreement' and 'disagreement' is absolute—one recalls Wittgenstein's saying at 4.023 that the only alternatives are *yes* and *no*.

The ground is now prepared for the picture theory of the proposition itself. Thesis 4.01, already quoted, asserts 'A proposition is a picture of reality', and the main steps by which Wittgenstein arrives at it consist in the two theses, also already quoted, that 'A logical picture of facts is a thought' (T 3) and a proposition is an expression of a thought (T 3.1). Wittgenstein now gives an account of what 4.01 means.

At first sight, he says, propositions do not seem to be pictures at all; but then at first sight musical notation does not appear to be a picture of music, and the alphabet does not seem to be a picture of speech; 'and yet these sign-languages prove to be pictures, even in the ordinary sense, of what they represent' (T 4.011). The musical analogy particularly well expresses Wittgenstein's point:

4.014 A gramophone record, the musical idea, the written notes, and the sound waves, all stand to one another in the same internal relation of depicting that holds between language and the world.

They are all constructed according to a common logical plan.

That this is so can be seen by noting that there are rules which enable a musician to translate a musical score into movements of his fingers on the keyboard, and thence, by means of the piano's mechanism, into sounds. Similarly, the structure of the grooves on a gramophone record are precisely correlative with the sounds which are produced when the record is played; and someone suitably trained could listen to the record and transcribe the music back into notation. The grooves, the sounds, the notation all have the same logical form. There is an *essential* connection between them, and that connection is their shared logical form. Wittgenstein says that just in the way a musical score depicts the sounds heard when it is played, so a proposition is a picture of reality in virtue of the same internal relation of shared logical form.

4.021   A proposition is a picture of reality: for if I understand a proposition, I know the situation that it represents.

4.03   A proposition communicates a situation to us and so it must be *essentially* connected with the situation.
And the connection is precisely that it is its logical picture.

This explains what Wittgenstein meant by saying, in 4.022 quoted earlier, 'A proposition *shows* its sense.' The concept of sense is what would colloquially be explained as 'meaning': the sense (meaning) of a proposition is the fact it pictures:

4.031   Instead of 'This proposition has such and such a sense', we can simply say 'This proposition represents such and such a situation.'

And what is meant by 'represents' here is straightforward. In talking of pictures *representing* reality Wittgenstein earlier says: 'What a picture represents [portrays, depicts, shows] is its sense'; thus, the sense of a proposition is the situation in reality which it depicts.

The final step in this account consists in Wittgenstein's tying together his theses about the structure of language, the structure of the world, and the picture theory:

4.0311 One name stands for one thing, another for another thing, and they are combined with one another. In this way the whole group—like a *tableau vivant*—presents a state of affairs.

4.0312 The possibility of propositions is based on the principle that objects have signs as their representatives.

From what has gone before, the import of these remarks is clear; it establishes the link between the 'elements'—names and objects—on which the picturing relation ultimately rests.

That, then, is the central argument of the *Tractatus*. Upon it rest the theses which it is Wittgenstein's overall aim to establish. These, it will be remembered, are that the only significant propositions (and hence thoughts) are those which are pictures of reality—that is, which are pictures of how things are in the world. And this in turn is to say that the only significant discourse is *factual discourse* (the 'propositions of natural science'). This has to be so, on Wittgenstein's theory, because if sense (colloquially, 'meaning') attaches to propositions only in virtue of their being pictures of reality—and reality is the sum of facts, that is, the existing states of affairs (whose existence determines what is *not* the case too, so that reality is complete and determinate)—then attempts to talk and think about what does not fall within the realm of facts literally *has no sense*, because such thought and talk does not picture anything: there *is* nothing for them to picture. The most significant consequence of this—a point familiar by now—is that nothing can be said about ethics, religion, and the problems of life; but before examining this consequence it is important to note another, namely the position in which Wittgenstein's theory leaves philosophy and logic.

The problem here is this. Because only factual discourse has sense, and because the propositions of philosophy and logic are not factual propositions, it follows that the propositions of philosophy and logic which Wittgenstein uses to state his theory are themselves senseless. His theory therefore appears paradoxical. But Wittgenstein is aware of this, and in response gives an account of what philosophy is and, separately, an account of the status of logic. Concerning philosophy he says:

4.111 Philosophy is not one of the natural sciences.
4.112 Philosophy aims at the logical clarification of thoughts.
Philosophy is not a body of doctrine but an activity.
A philosophical work consists essentially of elucidations.

> Philosophy does not result in 'philosophical proposi-
> tions' but rather in the clarification of propositions.
> Without philosophy thoughts are, as it were, cloudy
> and indistinct: its task is to make them clear and to
> give them sharp boundaries.

4.114　It must set limits to what can be thought; and, in doing
　　　so, to what cannot be thought.

4.115　It will signify what cannot be said, by presenting clearly
　　　what can be said.

The task Wittgenstein allots to philosophy therefore is
'elucidation', which is the process of clarifying our thought and
talk. And, consistently, this is just what the *Tractatus* aims to
do; in the last two quoted theses 'it' could just as well refer to
the *Tractatus* itself as to philosophy. In 4.114 Wittgenstein
adds: '[Philosophy] must set limits to thought by working
outwards through what can be thought.' This process of
'working outwards' by means of elucidations or clarifications
results, in Wittgenstein's view, in the attainment of a point of
vantage from which one can survey the limits of meaningful
discourse, and from which we can therefore recognize, for
exactly what they are, the steps which brought us there:

6.54　My propositions serve as elucidations in the following
　　　way: anyone who understands me eventually
　　　recognizes them as nonsensical, when he has used
　　　them—as steps—to climb up beyond them. (He must,
　　　so to speak, throw away the ladder after he has climbed
　　　up it.)
　　　　He must transcend these propositions, and then he
　　　will see the world aright.

Logic is in a different case. It will be remembered that the
truth-values of ordinary propositions depend upon those of
their constituent elementary propositions, in just the way
described by means of truth-tables in the preceding section.
Accordingly, ordinary propositions will sometimes be true and
sometimes false depending upon how things stand in the
world. But the true propositions of logic are *always* true, no

matter what the distribution of truth-values among their constituents; and propositions which are logically false are *always* false, no matter what the truth-values of their constituents. The former are *tautologies*, the latter *contradictions* (T 4.46). Accordingly, the truth-value of logical propositions is independent of how things are in the world: in Wittgenstein's characterization they 'say nothing' (T 6.11).

It does not follow that logic is vacuous. On the contrary, it has an important role as the instrument used in describing the fundamental structure of world and language, which Wittgenstein describes by saying 'the propositions of logic describe the scaffolding of the world'; and they do this by showing *what has to be the case* for language to have sense (T 6.124). All that logic presupposes is that names denote objects and propositions have sense (ibid.); otherwise 'logic has nothing to do with [questions about what] our world really is like' (T 6.1233). But although the task performed by logic is the wholly general and formal one of showing what the structures of world and language have to be in order for them to connect, it is crucial; for it thereby shows what the limits of meaningful discourse are.

Since, as we have seen, those limits enclose factual discourse only, everything to do with value and religion falls outside them. Accordingly, nothing can be *said* about these matters. But they are what is truly important; Wittgenstein describes them as 'what is higher' (T 6.42), and both in the *Tractatus* and in several letters he emphasizes the point that they are what the *Tractatus* is, in the end, really about—even though this is shown by the *Tractatus*'s being (almost) *silent* about them. To understand this one must grasp a point which Wittgenstein emphasizes in connection with his main argument and his view of philosophy as 'elucidation'. This is that one cannot properly use langauge to talk about language; one cannot properly *say* that propositions have a certain structure the elements of which are linked, through the picturing relation, with elements of the world. Of course, this is exactly what the *Tractatus* is largely about; but the propositions of the *Tractatus*, which are philosophical and therefore elucidatory propositions, are steps of a discardable ladder, as we have just seen. Strictly, the logical structures of language, world, and their relation *show* themselves or make themselves *manifest* when one sees them aright: Wittgenstein puts this by saying: 'Propositions cannot represent logical form: it is mirrored in them. What finds its reflection in language, language cannot represent' (T 4.121). Now, in just the same way, one cannot say things of an ethical or religious nature, for these matters lie outside the limits of language and therefore there is nothing for propositions about them to picture—which means that such propositions cannot have sense. Rather, the ethical and religious *show themselves*: 'There are indeed things that cannot be put into words. They *make themselves manifest*. They are what is mystical' (T 6.522).

One possible explanation of Wittgenstein's intentions here is that he is seeking to protect matters of value from the debunking encroachments of science. Science deals with the world—the realm of facts—and how things are in the world is *contingent*, that is, accidental; things happen to be the way they are in the world, and might well have been otherwise (T 6.41). But matters of value cannot be accidental, Wittgenstein says; they are too important (ibid.). Since the realms of fact and value are utterly distinct, the propositions of the former cannot be used to describe or explain anything to do with the latter. The latter transcend—that is, lie beyond the limits of—the world.

Wittgenstein does not however restrict himself to these negative points. In a few brief and unsystematic remarks occupying the last four pages of the *Tractatus* he indicates what he thinks the ethical and religious show of themselves. He says that good or bad acts of the will make no difference to the world, in the sense that they do not change any facts about how things are in the world, but rather that they alter 'the limits of the world' (T 6.43), that is, they affect how the world *as a whole* appears to the moral agent. Accordingly, to the good-willed agent the world appears 'altogether different' from the world of the bad-willed agent (ibid.). Wittgenstein then says: 'The world of the happy man is a different one from that of the unhappy man' (ibid.). This suggests either that goodwilling produces or is attended by happiness for the good-willed agent,

and the opposite for the bad-willed agent; or that the
fundamental moral good is happiness itself. The latter
interpretation has commended itself to some commentators,
but the former appears to be better supported by what
Wittgenstein says in the accompanying discussion: in a remark
shortly preceding T 6.43 he says that ethical reward and
punishment must reside in actions themselves, and are not to
be thought of in association with their consequences in the
realm of facts, which is the 'usual sense' of the terms
'punishment' and 'reward' (T 6.422). The thought therefore
seems to be that goodwilling contains its own reward—
happiness—and badwilling the converse.

Wittgenstein's view that matters of value concern the world
as a whole, and not matters of fact within it, is reinforced by
his remarks about death and God. At my death, he says, the
world does not change for me, but ends (T 6.431); therefore my
own death is not an event in my life—'we do not live to
experience death'—and in a sense therefore 'Our life has no end
in just the way our visual field has no limits' (T 6.4311). Again,
concerning God, he says 'How things are in the world is a
matter of complete indifference to what is higher. God does not
reveal himself *in* the world' (T 6.432). This remark says that
considerations about God, as perhaps the source or focus of
value, are solely related to the world as a whole, just as with
matters of value themselves. Two propositions bear this out:

6.44   It is not *how* things are in the world that is mystical,
        but *that* it exists.
6.45   To view the world *sub specie aeterni* is to view it as a
        whole—a limited whole.
        Feeling the world as a limited whole—it is this that is
        mystical.

These remarks lead up to the famous last sentence of the
Tractatus—'Whereof we cannot speak, thereof we must be
silent' (T 7)—and Wittgenstein asserts this for the now familiar
reason that since ethical and religious matters lie outside the
world, nothing can be said about them. This, Wittgenstein says
in his letters, is the *real* point of his argument, arrived at by

means of a logical investigation into the nature of language, world, and their connection.

3 *Some comments and questions*

The *Tractatus* has had a curious fate. It is treated as a work of historical interest rather than as an argument requiring the challenge and testing which philosophical theses usually receive. It is often expounded, explained, and interpreted, but it is rarely criticized in a serious way. For this there are good reasons. The chief of them has to do with the *Tractatus*'s place in Wittgenstein's philosophical development: it is an early work, and it was in effect repudiated by its author—indeed Wittgenstein came to make a rejection of its central doctrines the very cornerstone of his later philosophy. Few of its ideas, accordingly, are treated as genuine candidates for adoption or rejection. And this is why commentators, although they recognize a need to explain the *Tractatus*, very rarely offer a critical assessment of it. In certain respects the *Tractatus* is like the game of chess. One cannot imagine thinking that the *Tractatus* might be *true* any more than one can imagine thinking that a game of chess might be true. This is because the *Tractatus* is an uninterpreted calculus. The key notions—'object', 'name', and so on—are formal devices like the pieces in chess: the 'queen' in chess is not in any sense a *queen*, even a toy one, but is a purely formal entity defined by its permitted moves alone. This is what the 'objects' and 'names' of the *Tractatus* are; they are elements of abstract parallel structures, defined only by their roles and mutual relations. The 'names' and 'objects' of the *Tractatus* are very remote from being *names* (like 'Tom') and *objects* (like teacups)—as remote as a chess queen is from being a queen.

When, however, one turns to giving a critical assessment of the *Tractatus*, as Wittgenstein himself did, it quickly becomes apparent that there are many reasons for calling its doctrines into question. Some, briefly, are as follows.

The first is a criticism which Wittgenstein himself came to level at the *Tractatus* and which prompted him to take a quite different approach in his major later work, the *Philosophical Investigations*. It is this: the *Tractatus* has a symmetry, neatness, and apparent rigour of just the kind which makes, say, an elegant proof in mathematics so pleasing to the intellect. But it has this character at too high a cost, for what its symmetry and appearance of rigour result in is a huge oversimplification of the issues with which it deals. This comes out in a number of ways.

First, Wittgenstein assumed in the *Tractatus* that language has a single essence which he could specify by unearthing its logical structure. The tendentious concepts are those of *the* essence and of *the* logical form of language. The idea that language has a unitary nature which can be captured in a single formula, identifying which provides at a stroke solutions to all philosophical problems about thought, the world, value, religion, truth, and more, is an extraordinarily ambitious one— but it is what the early Wittgenstein asks us to accept. In the *Philosophical Investigations* Wittgenstein rejects this oversimplification and argues the opposite—that language is a vast collection of *different* activities each with its own logic. What the theory of the *Tractatus* offers in effect is a badly distorted view of language. Wittgenstein is there committed to saying that language is the sum total of propositions, where by 'propositions' he means what is asserted by declarative sentences like 'the table is brown', 'it is raining'—that is, statements of fact. But to think that language is employed exclusively to make statements is to ignore a host of other uses of language—questioning, commanding, exhorting, warning, promising, and much else besides. None of these uses can be explained in terms of the *Tractatus*'s account of language structure and the way sense attaches to propositions by means of the picturing relation. On the *Tractatus*'s principles, because questions, commands, promises, and the rest are not propositions, and hence not pictures of facts, they are senseless. But since these large areas of language are far from being senseless, a theory is needed which will take them properly into account.

In short, the *Tractatus* wholly neglects the great *variety* of language upon which Wittgenstein, in his later philosophy, insists; and this makes it possible to accept the theory of the *Tractatus* for a small fragment of language only. But even in the case of that fragment—the propositions expressed by declarative sentences—Wittgenstein came to reject his *Tractatus* view, for this was that the ultimate word-world link is the relation of denotation, the claim being that the *meaning* of a name is the object it denotes. Such a view will not bear scrutiny either, for reasons to be discussed later; Wittgenstein indeed opens the *Philosophical Investigations* with a lengthy refutation of it. And so the *Tractatus*'s theory of language, as Wittgenstein himself came to argue, is simplistic and distorting, and has therefore to be rejected.

It might fairly be asked why Wittgenstein—and others, Russell among them—did not see this at the time the *Tractatus* was written. The answer is that Wittgenstein—like those others—was beguiled into thinking about language and the world in terms of a particular model. This was the *atomistic* model. Wittgenstein's thesis rests on the assumption that language and the world are complex and hence structured, and that therefore their structures can be analysed into their simplest and most basic elements (or at least into simpler and more basic ones). He also assumes that logic—the logic described in section 1 above—is tailor-made for describing and analysing these structures. With these assumptions go others; for example, that language can be treated as a truth-functional structure—and it is easy to live with this particular assumption only if one thinks that all language consists in proposition-asserting declarative sentences (or at least, that all sentences can be turned into them).

These and allied assumptions raise a number of important questions. Is it clear that the logic of Frege and Russell is peculiarly the right one for analysing language and the world? Other candidates for 'the logic of natural language' have been proposed. This prompts doubts of the kind Wittgenstein himself later felt about what if anything is meant by talk of '*the* logical form of language'. In any case, do language and the world have 'underlying structures' which are different from their surface structures? If so, is it clear that these underlying structures are anything like they are said to be in the *Tractatus*? Why indeed should we accept Wittgenstein's pronouncements on this matter in the *Tractatus*'s early part?—for he gives no *argument* there to show that this view of language and the world is correct.

In the *Tractatus* Wittgenstein offers no account or defence of any of his basic assumptions, almost all of which, as we see from these examples, very much require both. The concepts of analysis, logical form, Frege–Russell logic—all these and more hang together in a pattern which makes doctrines like those of the *Tractatus* and Russell's 'Logical Atomism' inevitable as an outcome if one accepts and works with them. The application of these concepts in Russell's work, given his interest in how they connect with the everyday matters of perceiving, judging, knowing, determining truth, and so on, results in a more concrete (although, in the end, no more acceptable) theory than Wittgenstein offers; it is Wittgenstein's wholly abstract use of them which issues in the chess-like character of the *Tractatus* theory. But the most important point is the one selected by Wittgenstein himself for particular attack when he came to work out his later philosophy, namely the fact that the *Tractatus* oversimplifies and distorts language. And it does this by claiming that language is the sum of propositions, that it has a single essence, that this essence is describable in terms of predicate logic, that language and world have parallel structures which connect by means of the picturing relationship, and that sense attaches to what we say (and therefore think) only if what we say is a picture of a fact. Wittgenstein came to reject all this.

Even were we to ignore the foregoing remarks, however, we would find other difficulties in the theory of the *Tractatus*. It is as we have seen a theory about the connection of language and the world; but, as we have also seen, in setting it out Wittgenstein refuses to specify what he means by 'names', 'objects', 'elementary propositions', and 'states of affairs'—and we can now look at a simple but important reason why it matters that these notions have been left unexplained.

On the *Tractatus* view, a proposition is true if it 'pictures' or corresponds to what is the case. As it stands this seems to be an unexceptionable characterization of what it is for a proposition to be true; but a little probing reveals trouble. Leaving the *Tractatus* aside for a moment, suppose we consider the proposition 'the cat is on the mat', asserted when a given real cat is on a real mat. What is the structure of the proposition? What is the structure of the fact? How exactly do they 'correspond'? We might—setting aside problems about 'denotation' itself—be tempted to analyse the proposition into two denoting terms and a relational expression, or even into three denoting terms with 'is on' denoting a *relation* and not a *thing*; but there is no such apparently ready way with the fact, since there are only two *things* present—the cat and the mat—and it is hard to see how the relation between them is a *constituent* of the fact in the same way that the cat and the mat are, for these latter are concrete entities whereas relations are abstract. At the very outset, then, facts and their correspondent propositions are awkward to analyse into their constituents because it is unclear what is to count as a 'constituent'. In the case of a proposition like 'the car is blue' the problem comes into even sharper focus, for here on the face of it there are two propositional constituents, namely, a subject and a predicate, but just one blue car—unless one chooses to think that the fact in which the existence of a blue car consists is somehow composed of a car and a blueness, say—a thing and a property. But this will not do; why not say that the fact is composed of a car, a blueness, and four 'tyrenesses'—or any other combination of items and properties one cares to think of?

These remarks are cursory, but they are enough to show that when one reflects on the theory of the *Tractatus* it becomes extraordinarily hard to see what the 'psychological' enquiry left aside by Wittgenstein could yield in the way of candidates for objects, names, and the rest. One example shows why. In the cat-on-the-mat case, the thought was that the word 'cat' might denote an object, namely the cat. But the word 'cat' cannot serve as a *name* in the *Tractatus*'s sense, nor a cat as an 'object', for cats are complex, analysable things—they are, as it were, states of affairs—whereas objects are simple, unchanging, and unanalysable. Since cats are not objects, 'cat' cannot on the *Tractatus* theory be a name. But then—and here is our 'chess' difficulty concerning the *Tractatus*—what *are* the 'names' and 'objects'? In the absence of any indication it is impossible to know whether the picture theory of the relation between language and the world is even half-way plausible: yet this is the centrepiece of the *Tractatus* theory. This is not a minor cavil. It says that when one stays within the circle of Wittgenstein's key concepts an impression of informativeness subsists—but any probing, or any attempt to relate them to more concrete matters, seems to leave one with a piece of useless conceptual apparatus.

Part of the problem here is connected with a more general one, which is that the *Tractatus* contains few *arguments*. Its theses are asserted, and the support or supplement they get is various: sometimes an illustration, sometimes an expansion or a definition; often a metaphor or simile. These occur much more frequently than do arguments or proofs of the kind standardly employed in philosophical discussion. At crucial points the only explanation offered for important theses is a figure of speech, as with the key remarks about the picturing relation—'*That* is how a picture is attached to reality: it reaches right out to it' (T 2.1511); 'It is laid against reality like a ruler' (T 2.1512); 'These correlations are, as it were, the feelers of the picture's elements with which the picture touches reality' (T 2.1515). It is of course true that in Wittgenstein's view philosophy consists in giving 'elucidations', and does not consist in 'propositions' in the *Tractatus*'s sense; but a reader might have grounds for thinking that nothing has been elucidated if the most important concepts deployed—as with 'names' and 'objects'—have been left un-interpreted, so that he cannot grasp what moves have been made by their employment; or if talk of crucial aspects of the theory—as with 'picturing'—proceeds in terms of metaphors in which pictures have 'feelers', or similes in which a picture is 'like a ruler . . . laid against reality'. These considerations are important for an assessment of the *Tractatus*. In connection with the theses about language and its picturing relation to the world, the consequence is that once one has stepped back from the architectonic issues, and begun to try to make working sense of the theory (to 'see the world aright' in Wittgenstein's words), the project turns out to be unfeasible: for, quite literally, one does not know what Wittgenstein takes himself to be talking about.

Something like this difficulty infects Wittgenstein's closing remarks about matters of value also. Ramsey remarked that to describe ethics as 'nonsense but important nonsense' is too like having one's cake and eating it. His comment touches a nerve. Wittgenstein accords to value a transcendent and detached character which fits ill with the fact that ethical concerns are anything *but* thus detached: morally problematic situations arise every day, and the sense in which they are problematic is in important part a matter of what the facts are in those situations. For example, our judging that it is immoral to inflict gratuitous pain upon animals rests in important part on facts about the capacity of animals to feel pain (there is nothing immoral, by contrast, about kicking a stone); so here the contingent facts about how things are in the world make a difference to our actions—our practice—in the affairs of daily life. Moreover, if it were true that value somehow just 'manifested itself', as Wittgenstein says it does, it would be puzzling why conflicts and disagreements should arise over ethical questions, or why people can passionately and sincerely hold views which are quite opposite to those held with equal passion and sincerity by others.

There are other more detailed criticisms one might urge against the *Tractatus* were there space to pursue them. A point which should be stressed, however, is that although Wittgenstein was unsparing of his earlier self in rejecting or emending that self's commitments, this does not mean that his later outlook is entirely opposed to his earlier one; there are continuities as well as changes between the two phases of his thought, as we shall see.

4 *The influence of the early philosophy*

On the standard view of Wittgenstein's early philosophical influence it is held that the *Tractatus* constituted a major source of inspiration for 'Logical Positivism', the theory developed by the Vienna Circle. In line with this view a writer on the recent history of philosophy, J. O. Urmson, is able to say, without feeling the need to qualify, that some of the Circle's views were 'based largely on Wittgenstein's *Tractatus*, by which they had been profoundly influenced'. There are many similar statements in other writings about the period. In addition, the standard view has it that the influence was a one-way affair; commentators on Wittgenstein's later philosophy make little of the supposition that the changes which occurred in his thought during the 1920s and especially 1930s, many of them radical, resulted in any way from his contacts with the Circle and its ideas.

More recent studies suggest that the relationship between Wittgenstein's early work and that of the Circle was by no means so straightforward. That there *was* a connection is not in doubt; but it seems that Wittgenstein's influence was much less than has been supposed, being exercised in the main on just two of the Circle's members, who however did not as a result come to disagree with the rest of the Circle (except on certain points largely independent of Wittgenstein's theories).

These matters will be discussed shortly. First, it is important to note a much earlier effect of Wittgenstein's work, one which manifested itself years before the *Tractatus* was published. This was Wittgenstein's influence on Russell. The biographical remarks in Chapter 1 above show how Wittgenstein was led to study under Russell as a result of reading Russell's *Principles of Mathematics*. That book, and the *Principia Mathematica* which Russell wrote with Whitehead, had an enormous effect on Wittgenstein; the *Tractatus* indeed owes its existence and many of its ideas to them. But in working with Russell at Cambridge during 1912–13 Wittgenstein quickly ceased to be a pupil, and the discussions between them resulted in their each developing views which, although rather different in completed form (the *Tractatus* and Russell's *Lectures on Logical Atomism* of 1918), share certain fundamentals and a common starting-point in the conception of logic as revealing the structure of language and the world. So far as the fundamentals and the starting-point are concerned, Russell is the main source. (Those who have some knowledge of philosophy would recognize that Russell had himself been influenced by his first-hand study of Frege and Leibniz; and to these influences, which give rise to the logical and metaphysical aspects of Russell's work, must be added that of Hume, from whom Russell's epistemology in large part derives. Wittgenstein accordingly inherits these influences through Russell. His other influences are Schopenhauer and, through him, Kant.) But Wittgenstein's responses to what he learned from Russell in their turn influenced the development of the latter's thought, and it is this reciprocity which makes for the points of similarity between their views in the next several years. When Russell published his *Lectures on Logical Atomism* he described the theses they contain as having been 'learned from my friend Wittgenstein', a characteristically generous remark which in fact overstates the debt, since most of what is essential to Russell's views in the *Lectures* is already to be found in work published before he met Wittgenstein.

One major result of Wittgenstein's influence was that Russell left unpublished a book he was writing when Wittgenstein first came to Cambridge. It was to have been called *Theory of Knowledge*. Only its first six chapters saw light of day, in the form of articles; Russell abandoned the rest as a result of Wittgenstein's hostility to it. In a letter to a friend, written in 1913, Russell reported what had happened: 'We were both cross from the heat. I showed [Wittgenstein] a crucial part of what I had been writing. He said it was all wrong, not realising the difficulties—that he had tried my view and knew it wouldn't work. I couldn't understand his objection—in fact he was very inarticulate—but I feel in my bones that he must be right, and he has seen something that I have missed'. (It appears from memoirs of Wittgenstein that this procedure of demolishing someone's views—and confidence—more by the manner than the content of his opposition was characteristic of him throughout his life.) The relinquishing of so substantial a project by Russell testifies to his estimation of Wittgenstein at the time and the nature of the intellectual relations between them. The forfeiture of Russell's book must count as Wittgenstein's first effect on philosophy.

As indicated, the question of Wittgenstein's relations with the Vienna Circle are less straightforward to describe. The Circle in great measure owed its existence to Moritz Schlick, who arrived in Vienna in 1922 as Professor in the philosophy of inductive science. What began as a discussion group became in due course more organized, with a programme of research and a journal, *Erkenntnis*, to publish its results. The Circle had among its members a number of extremely able people; apart from Schlick himself there were, for example, Rudolf Carnap, Otto Neurath, and Hans Reichenbach. The group met for over ten years from the mid-1920s onwards, and broke up as a result of its members being driven into exile by Fascism.

Central to the doctrine propounded by members of the Circle—'Logical Positivism'—is the requirement that a line of demarcation be drawn between science and what the Circle's members, giving the word a pejorative connotation, labelled 'metaphysics' (in their usage a synonym for 'nonsense'). They did this by saying that only propositions concerned with matters of fact or with logical relations between concepts are meaningful. Propositions not falling into either of these two classes—the propositions of ethics and religion, for example— they regarded as expressions having emotional or exhortatory but not cognitive content; strictly, they lack sense. Factual propositions, they said, are based upon experience, and are significant because they can be verified or falsified by experience. The other class of significant propositions—those concerning logical relations between concepts—they called 'analytic' propositions, and defined them as those whose truth-value can be determined simply by inspecting the meaning of the words (or symbols) in which they consist. These include the propositions of logic and mathematics. And the Positivists held that the purpose of philosophy is to clarify the propositions of empirical science by means of logical analysis of meaning, with philosophy so conceived counting as part of science and not as an independent discipline.

On the face of it there is much common ground between these views and what is said in the *Tractatus*. Wittgenstein talks of propositions as pictures of facts; of logic as tautological or 'analytic'; of philosophy's role being confined to 'elucidations'; and of the nonsensicality of all propositions other than those of natural science, logic and mathematics. These apparent similarities led the Circle's members to study the *Tractatus* carefully at their meetings in 1925 and 1926, and prompted Schlick to arrange discussions with Wittgenstein. Schlick's wife has left a record of the excitement her husband felt after his first encounter with Wittgenstein in 1927. For a time Wittgenstein had talks with other members of the Circle also, among them Carnap and Feigl; but soon his regular contacts were limited to Schlick and an associate of Schlick's called Friedrich Waismann. Although Wittgenstein left Vienna for Cambridge in 1929 he frequently returned for visits, and on these occasions as well as by letter his relations with Schlick and Waismann were maintained. This lasted until Schlick was murdered by a student (probably for political reasons) on the steps of Vienna University in 1936.

Wittgenstein's contacts with Schlick and Waismann were therefore considerable. The latter kept a record of their discussions with Wittgenstein in the years 1929–31 which has been published. Schlick encouraged Wittgenstein to collaborate with Waismann on a book explaining the *Tractatus*'s doctrines together with the developments in Wittgenstein's thought since its publication. Waismann was to write it under Wittgenstein's guidance. When by the early 1930s it became clear that Wittgenstein's thought had changed too much for that project to be worthwhile, Schlick kept the plan alive by persuading Wittgenstein to let Waismann present his new views instead. Waismann laboured under Wittgenstein's changes of mind throughout these years, rarely to the latter's satisfaction; the resultant book was published under Waismann's own name much later, in 1967, six years after its author's death. During the period of collaboration between Wittgenstein and Waismann, however, Waismann published aspects of Wittgenstein's newly emerging views in several lectures and articles.

Although Wittgenstein's contacts with these two members of the Circle were extensive, they did not have much effect on Schlick's Positivism. As with others of the Circle, Schlick's views were established before he met Wittgenstein; their sources lay in Hume, Ernst Mach, and the empiricist tradition of philosophy, together with the logic of Russell and Frege (the Circle's other leader, Carnap, had studied with Frege at Jena in the years 1910–14). By the time the Circle was established as a group with a definite identity and research programme, therefore, its basic Positivist tenets were well entrenched. Moreover, a number of the Circle's members, particularly

Carnap and Reichenbach, have left accounts of Wittgenstein's effect on the Circle which show that the *Tractatus*'s impact was minor and even, in some ways, negative. At the 1925–6 meetings when the *Tractatus* was being discussed Neurath constantly interjected 'Metaphysics!'—as noted, a Positivist term of abuse—and in a letter to Waismann some years later Neurath wrote: 'The Wittgenstein period took you (and to some extent Schlick as well) away from our common task.' Carnap wrote in his intellectual autobiography: 'I had erroneously believed that [Wittgenstein's] attitude to metaphysics was similar to ours. I had not paid sufficient attention to the statements in his book, because his feelings and thoughts in this area were too divergent from mine.'

The most telling evidence for determining the extent of Wittgenstein's effect on the Vienna Circle lies not so much in the reports and recollections of its members as in their publications and the doctrines advanced in them. The books and papers which flowed from the Circle reveal not just that Wittgenstein's influence was minimal but that it could not have been otherwise, for there are many deep differences between the theses of the *Tractatus* and those of Logical Positivism. The chief of these is evident, first, in the Positivists' view that the foundations of factual knowledge lie in empirical observation (later modified by Neurath and Carnap, in opposition to the others, into a form of 'coherence' theory in which the basic propositions are determined by theoretical needs rather than by 'raw observation'); secondly, in the Positivists' theories of probability and induction, to which they accorded great importance; thirdly, in the marginal position accorded by Positivism to matters of value and religion—most of the Positivists were scornful of religion, regarding it as primitive superstition, whereas Wittgenstein throughout his life retained the deepest respect for it; fourthly, in the Positivists' belief in the 'unity of science', which, as Waismann's records show, Wittgenstein found conceptually unattractive; and in a number of other detailed respects besides.

What indeed the evidence suggests is that it was Wittgenstein who was influenced by the Circle's ideas rather more than the converse—not in the sense that he came to be, except rather briefly, something of a Positivist himself, but *negatively*, in that he came to put progressively greater distance between himself and those tenets in the *Tractatus* which were, however superficially, similar to the Positivists' outlook, as if a greater realization of its Positivistic elements persuaded him that the *Tractatus* was in important respects mistaken. Writing to Schlick in 1932 Wittgenstein says: 'There are *many, many* formulations in that book [the *Tractatus*] that I am no longer in agreement with', and this sentiment is emphasized in Waismann's record of Wittgenstein's conversations. At least part of the impetus to Wittgenstein's later philosophy is accordingly the result of his learning from the Positivists what he could no longer agree with in his own earlier work.

One of the things which may have led commentators to overstate Wittgenstein's effect on the Circle is that in his conversations with Schlick and Waismann in the late 1920s— when Wittgenstein himself was in his most Positivist phase as a result of Schlick's influence on him—he gave neat formulation to a principle already espoused by the Positivists, namely that 'the meaning of a statement is its method of verification', which is to say that a statement's sense consists in the methods employed to determine whether it is true or false. This idea, on an interpretation which Wittgenstein was then prepared to give of the *Tractatus*'s doctrines, accords with his view that propositions are true or false depending upon whether or not they correctly picture the facts. Schlick made much of Wittgenstein's way of stating the principle; when A. J. Ayer publicized the Circle's ideas in English in his *Language, Truth and Logic* (1936) the verification principle occupied pride of place and excited much debate. But it was the form of words rather than the conception which Wittgenstein contributed; and he did not share the verificationist outlook, at least in its blunt Positivistic version, for long.

For the foregoing among other reasons it is no longer possible to think of the *Tractatus* as having inspired a philosophical movement, as most earlier commentators claimed. This does not however mean that the *Tractatus* is a negligible work historically. It has interest because it is an uncompromising, indeed an extreme, example of 'logical atomism', and therefore shows with some vividness what that species of view can involve. But its chief importance resides in its being the source, in part positively and in larger part negatively, for Wittgenstein's own later philosophy, developed from the early 1930s onwards. To this we now turn.

3 The later philosophy

The topic of this chapter is Wittgenstein's mature work, contained in his writings from the mid-1930s until his death in 1951. In the half decade prior to this, however, Wittgenstein's thought went through a period of transition in which the themes of the later philosophy emerged from his reconsideration of the *Tractatus*. I begin by sketching this transition briefly.

In the following sections most of what is central to Wittgenstein's later philosophy is canvassed. I have, however, omitted specific consideration of his philosophy of mathematics and the shorter posthumously published writings; Wittgenstein's position is essentially the same in these as in the chief works considered below, which are the *Philosophical Investigations*, *Zettel*, and *On Certainty*.

1 *The transitional period*

Part of the story about the development of Wittgenstein's later philosophy is told in the last section, dealing with the contacts between Wittgenstein and the Vienna Circle. As suggested there, in the years during which he had discussions with members of the Circle Wittgenstein began by maintaining his early views, went through a phase of giving them a Positivistic interpretation, and then—in the early 1930s—came to think them wrong in a number of important respects. After his return to Cambridge in 1929 Wittgenstein embarked upon a period of intense intellectual activity during which he wrote a great deal. This transitional phase lasted approximately until 1935, by which time many of the ideas to be met with in the *Philosophical Investigations* and others of the late works had made their appearance in his manuscripts.

The writings of the transitional period are genuinely transitional, containing elements both of the early and the later views. One major theme in them concerns the philosophy of mathematics; specifically, questions about what *status* the propositions of mathematics have. Are mathematical propositions necessary truths? Can they be explained wholly in terms of logic? If not, what account is to be given of them? Together with and related to this issue there are long exploratory investigations of language and meaning, psychological concepts, and the concept of knowledge. These latter constitute the central themes of the later philosophy itself. For Wittgenstein scholars the transitional writings are a rich source of material, since they foreshadow and prepare the way for the later philosophy, and display a development of thought which contains much of interest.

Following the award of his Ph.D. degree in 1929 Wittgenstein applied for a five-year Fellowship at Trinity College, Cambridge. In support of his candidature he had to submit an extended sample of his current research in philosophy, and duly did so. The work was a manuscript constituting much of what has since been published (1975) in an English translation entitled *Philosophical Remarks*, but better known in the German original as *Philosophische Bemerkungen*, under which title it was published in 1964. It is evident from the fact that Wittgenstein wrote a Preface to the work that he intended to publish it. (Indeed, at various times throughout the remaining two decades of his life Wittgenstein had plans, and made arrangements, to publish various of his writings; letters between him and the Syndics of Cambridge University Press show that some of the plans came close to fulfilment. In the event none of Wittgenstein's writings were published until after his death, and the reason is that he was never quite content with how he had stated his views or ordered the remarks in which they were expressed.)

The *Philosophische Bemerkungen* was written in the period up to 1932, and it displays many signs of Wittgenstein's contacts with the Positivists and their influence upon him, particularly in the emphasis it places upon verification. It defends some of the *Tractatus*'s theses—for an important example, the picture theory—but new elements appear in its doing so, the chief of which anticipate concerns that were to occupy progressively more of Wittgenstein's attention as the years passed. One of the most important was the emphasis he placed on a conception of 'meaning as use', to be discussed in some detail below.

Between 1932 and 1934 Wittgenstein continued to write copiously, producing a large manuscript which was eventually published in 1969 as *Philosophische Grammatik* and in English in 1974 as *Philosophical Grammar*. The work has two parts, the titles of which—'The Proposition and its Sense' and 'On Logic and Mathematics' respectively—display its content. While revising the work in 1933–4 Wittgenstein dictated notes to his students which subsequently circulated in typescript form under the title *The Blue Book*, so called because of the colour of its binding. There is a great similarity between this samizdat publication and the first part of the *Philosophical Grammar*.

The importance of the *Grammar* resides in the fact that it contains, sometimes in preliminary form and sometimes in full, material which later appears in the *Philosophical Investigations*. The central question addressed in Part One of the *Grammar* concerns how it is that we attach meaning to the uttered sounds and inscribed marks which constitute language. In brief, Wittgenstein's argument here is as follows.

A natural view is to say that understanding language is a mental process which attends our linguistic activities. On such a view, when I speak, hear, or read, something goes on in my mind which constitutes 'grasping the meaning' of the signs being used. Wittgenstein argues against this view; he says that understanding language is not a *process* but an *ability*. One illustration he gives of this thesis concerns the matter of 'knowing how to play chess'. If knowing how to play chess were a process—that is, something going on in one's head— then it would be appropriate to ask: '*When* do you know how to play chess? All the time? Or just while you are making the move?' (*Phil. Gram.* §50). But these questions are manifestly odd; their unnatural character shows that it is a mistake to think of understanding and knowing as events in the mind. Wittgenstein says that we should think of them instead as capacities, as something we have a practical ability to do. In any case, he says, the notion of 'mental processes' is itself confused and liable to create misunderstandings—a claim which Wittgenstein regarded as very important and which therefore plays, as we shall see, a dominating role in the philosophical psychology of the later works.

Wittgenstein goes on in the *Grammar* to investigate the crucial notions of 'thinking' and 'understanding' themselves, doing so in ways which closely anticipate the *Investigations*, particularly in his arguing that there are many different kinds of understanding, linked not by their common possession of a set of essential or defining characteristics but by a general relationship of similarity which he calls 'family resemblance'. This concept also plays an important role in the *Investigations*. It appears first in the *Grammar*, and then more explicitly in *The Blue Book*. In this latter there is another significant development for the later philosophy and in particular the theory of meaning as use: Wittgenstein says that instead of asking, 'What is the meaning of a word?' we should ask, 'What is it to *explain* the meaning of a word? How is the use of a word learned?' And his response to the problem with which both *The Blue Book* and Part One of the *Grammar* deal, namely, what is it that 'gives life' (gives *meaning*) to the sounds and marks constituting language, is accordingly this: 'if we had to name anything as the life of the sign, we should have to say that it was its use' (*The Blue Book* p. 4).

In 1934–5 Wittgenstein dictated to two of his pupils a manuscript which, like *The Blue Book*, had a samizdat circulation at Cambridge and beyond. Again the colour of its binding determined its title, this time *The Brown Book*. In content it is very close to the *Investigations*; it is indeed a virtual draft of the latter work. Its appearance marks the end of the transitional phase in Wittgenstein's thought; thereafter the writings which develop the ideas of the *Grammar* and *Blue and Brown Books* constitute true drafts of the *Investigations*, as G. H. von Wright has shown in his reconstruction of the steps by which that book emerged. A striking feature of the transitional works is that the topics they address are very much those of the *Tractatus*, 'the proposition and its sense' foremost among them—and this remains true throughout the later work; but increasingly there appears, together with these concerns and as a necessary adjunct of Wittgenstein's new way of dealing with them, discussion of psychological concepts such as *understanding*, *intending*, *experiencing*, and others. The reasons why will become apparent shortly.

In contemplating the publication of his *chef-d'œuvre*, the *Investigations*, Wittgenstein came to the view that it would be better understood if the *Tractatus* were published along with it. His reason was that the *Investigations* is in many important ways a reaction to the *Tractatus*, so that a comparison of the two forcefully illustrates what the *Investigations* has to say. The discussion of the later philosophy to which we now turn shows in what sense this is so.

2 *Method, meaning, and use*

In the *Tractatus* Wittgenstein's position was that language has a unique discoverable essence, a single underlying logic, which can be explained by means of a structure-revealing analysis of language and the world and a description of the relation—the 'picturing' relation—between them. The picturing relation itself rests, at bottom, on a denotative link between names and objects; names 'mean' objects. The argument of the *Investigations* is based on an explicit rejection of this view. Here Wittgenstein says that there is not *one* 'logic of language', but many; language has no single essence, but is a vast collection of different practices each with its own logic. Meaning does not consist in the denoting relation between words and things or in a picturing relation between propositions and facts; rather, the meaning of an expression is its *use* in the multiplicity of practices which go to make up language. Moreover, language is not something complete and autonomous which can be investigated independently of other considerations, for language is woven into all human activities and behaviour, and accordingly our many different uses of it are given content and significance by our practical affairs, our work, our dealings with one another and with the world we inhabit—a language, in short, is part of the fabric of an inclusive 'form of life'.

It is important to notice that in his transitional period Wittgenstein had come to a view of the nature of philosophical *method* which, while retaining central features of his

Tractatus view of philosophy, differs from it in a crucial respect. Understanding Wittgenstein's position on this matter does much to illuminate his later philosophical commitments.

As noted earlier, Wittgenstein's *Tractatus* view was that philosophical problems arise because we 'misunderstand the logic of our language'. This conviction remained with Wittgenstein throughout his philosophical work. What changed, as we have just seen, is his view about what is meant by 'the logic of language'. But there was another change also. Wittgenstein had come to think that the problems which arise because of our misunderstandings of language cannot be solved by constructing a systematic philosophical theory, as he had tried to do in the *Tractatus*. Instead of devising *theories* to deal with philosophical problems, he says, we should 'dissolve' those problems by removing the misunderstandings which cause them in the first place. We are thus to conceive of philosophy as a *therapeutic* enterprise in a quite literal sense: 'The philosopher's treatment of a question is like the treatment of an illness' (P 255). In the transitional and later works, accordingly, Wittgenstein abandons the rigorously systematic method of the *Tractatus* and adopts instead a piecemeal approach explicitly designed *not* to result in a structured theory. It is this which gives the later works their curiously disjointed and rambling appearance in contrast to the *Tractatus*'s austere architecture.

Wittgenstein's later view of the proper method and aims of philosophy is set out in the *Investigations*. Puzzles arise, Wittgenstein says, because of misuse of language or misconceptions about its nature. If we have an incorrect view of the way language works we shall be liable to confusions; for example, we shall assimilate the use of one kind of expression to that of quite a different kind, or we shall mistakenly try to understand an expression in isolation from the contexts in which it normally does its work. 'The confusions which occupy us', Wittgenstein says, 'arise when language is like an engine idling, not when it is doing work' (P 132); 'Philosophical problems arise when language *goes on holiday*' (P 38). The remedy is to look at how language *actually* works: '[Philosophical problems] are, of course, not empirical problems; they are solved, rather, by looking into the workings of our language, and that in such a way as to make us recognize those workings: *in despite of* an urge to misunderstand them' (P 109).

On this view philosophical problems will vanish when the workings of language are properly grasped. Until philosophers apply the remedy of 'looking into' those workings they are like flies trapped in a bottle, helplessly buzzing about. Wittgenstein remarks, 'What is your aim in philosophy? To shew the fly the way out of the fly-bottle.' And what is needed for this is a grasp of the difference between what Wittgenstein calls 'surface grammar' and 'depth grammar'. By 'grammar' he does not mean what is ordinarily understood by this term; rather, he means *logic*—more precisely, the logic of a given linguistic activity. There are many different kinds of linguistic activity; therefore there are many different ways in which the 'grammar' of language works. Philosophers become trapped in the fly-bottle, in Wittgenstein's view, as a result of noticing only 'surface grammar': 'In the use of words one might distinguish "surface grammar" from "depth grammar" . . . compare the depth grammar, say, of the word "to mean", with what its surface grammar would lead us to suspect. No wonder we find it difficult to know our way about' (P 664). Accordingly Wittgenstein calls the *Investigations* a 'grammatical' enquiry: 'Our investigation is therefore a grammatical one. Such an investigation sheds light on our problems by clearing misunderstandings away' (P 90). This harks back to the *Tractatus*'s description of philosophy as 'elucidation'—another case of continuity between Wittgenstein's early and later outlooks—but in the *Investigations* the method is intimately connected with the views advanced, in that the content of those views just *is*, in a sense, that method at work: for what Wittgenstein's remarks about method come down to is the claim that in philosophy we should not seek to *explain* but only to *describe* ('explaining' amounts to constructing further theories), for we are not trying to discover new information but, quite differently, to organize properly—and by so doing to make ourselves understand properly—what we already know about our language and thought.

What Wittgenstein says about method informs his entire approach in the later philosophy. The effect of that method's application becomes clear as one goes through the main ideas of the *Investigations*, as we shall now see.

The first step towards a grasp of the workings of language is taken, in Wittgenstein's *Investigations* view, by freeing ourselves from the beguiling but mistaken assumption that a unitary account of language can be given—that is, an account which explains the whole working of language in terms of a single theoretical model. His target here is of course the *Tractatus*; by attacking it he is able to present, in response, the *Investigations* view of language as a multiplicity of different activities. The attack on the *Tractatus* view of language is signalled in the Preface to the *Investigations*: '[Recently] I had occasion to re-read my first book . . . It suddenly seemed to me that I should publish these old thoughts and the new ones together: that the latter could be seen in the right light only by contrast with and against the background of my old way of thinking. For since beginning to occupy myself with philosophy again . . . I have been forced to recognize grave mistakes in what I wrote in that first book.'

Wittgenstein illustrates the 'grave mistakes' by reference not to the *Tractatus* itself but to St Augustine's account of language-learning in the *Confessions*. After quoting a number of lines from Augustine's text, among which occurs the sentence 'When my elders named some object . . . I grasped that the thing was called by the sound they uttered', Wittgenstein says: 'These words, it seems to me, give us a particular picture of human language. It is this: the individual words in language name objects—sentences are combinations of such names.—In this picture of language we find the roots of the following idea: Every word has a meaning. The meaning is correlated with the word. It is the object for which the word stands' (P 1). The theory just sketched is, of course, the *Tractatus* theory, but Wittgenstein uses Augustine's account to show that the conception of language at issue is both ancient and widespread. Moreover, this conception of language leads us, Wittgenstein says, to investigate language in the wrong way; we ask the wrong questions, specifically 'questions as to the *essence* of language, of propositions, of thought', and this mistakenly suggests that the 'essence' of language is 'not something that already lies open to view and that becomes surveyable by a rearrangement, but something that lies *beneath* the surface . . . "*the essence is hidden from us*": this is the form our problem . . . assumes' (P 92); and therefore 'We feel as if we had to *penetrate* phenomena' (P 90). And this in turn prompts commitment to the misleading model of language which Wittgenstein says St Augustine and the *Tractatus* share, for it 'come[s] to look as if [we should search for] something like a final analysis of our forms of language, and so a *single* completely resolved form of every expression. That is, as if our usual forms of expression were, essentially, unanalysed; as if there were something hidden in them that had to be brought to light' (P 91). Wittgenstein's response to this picture is unequivocal: it is to deny that there is any need to analyse, to 'discover the essence' lying hidden in discourse. 'Philosophy simply puts everything before us, and neither explains nor deduces anything.—Since everything lies open to view there is nothing to explain. For what is hidden, for example, is of no interest to us' (P 126). The key lies in a remark just quoted from P 92: the way language works *is*, Wittgenstein holds, 'something that already lies open to view, and that becomes surveyable by a rearrangement'.

What 'lies open to view', Wittgenstein says, is the fact that language is not *one uniform thing* but a host of different activities. We use language to describe, report, inform, affirm, deny, speculate, give orders, ask questions, tell stories, play-act, sing, guess riddles, make jokes, solve problems, translate, request, thank, greet, curse, pray, warn, reminisce, express emotions, and much else besides (compare especially P 23 and, for example, P 27, 180, 288, 654). All these different activities Wittgenstein calls 'language-games'. Earlier, in *The Brown Book*, he had used this notion to mean a simplified fragment of language, inspection of which tells us something about the nature of language proper. In the *Investigations* the label takes on a more general signification; it means any of the many and various language-using activities we engage in: 'the term "language-game" is meant to bring into prominence the fact

71

that the *speaking* of language is part of an activity, or of a form of life' (P 23). Wittgenstein talks of the 'multiplicity of language-games', and in P 23, directly after giving a list of language-games (much as set out above), says: 'It is interesting to compare the multiplicity of the tools in language and of the ways they are used, the multiplicity of kinds of words and sentences, with what logicians have said about the structure of language. (Including the author of the *Tractatus Logico-Philosophicus*.)' The comparison is one to be drawn between the great diversity of language-games and the false view of the 'logicians' and the *Tractatus*'s author that language has a *single* underlying logical structure.

Wittgenstein's use of the term 'game' is not intended to suggest that the different linguistic activities of reporting, describing, asking, and the rest are in some way frivolous or unimportant. They are, of course, earnest. His reason for employing the notion is given in this passage:

Consider . . . the proceedings we call 'games'. I mean board-games, card-games, ball games, Olympic games, and so on. What is common to them all?—Don't say: 'There must be something common or they would not all be called "games",' but *look* and *see* whether there is something common to *all*,—for if you look at them you will not see something that is in common to all, but similarities, relationships, and a whole series of them at that . . . And the result of this examination is: we see a complicated network of similarities overlapping and criss-crossing . . . I can think of no better expression to characterize these similarities than 'family resemblances'; for the various resemblances between members of a family: build, features, colour of eyes, gait, temperament, etc., etc., overlap and criss-cross in the same way.—And I shall say: 'games' form a family. (P 66–7)

The point Wittgenstein is urging in saying that *language* is a collection of language-games is as we have seen precisely that language has no single essence which can be unearthed and stated in terms of a unitary theory. To understand the workings of language we must first therefore recognize its variety and multiplicity—'Instead of producing something common to all that we call language, I am saying that these phenomena have no one thing in common which makes us use the same word for all,—but that they are *related* to one another in many different ways' (P 65). Once this is clear, in Wittgenstein's view, we see why it is wrong to think of meaning as he had thought of it in the *Tractatus*: there the claim was that the meaning of a word is the object it denotes; here, in the *Investigations*, it is that the meaning of an expression is the *use* to which it can be put in one or another of the many and various language-games constituting language: 'the meaning of a word is its use in the language' (P 43).

In the early sections of the *Investigations*, following his quotation from Augustine, Wittgenstein shows why the denotative theory of meaning adopted in the *Tractatus* is intrinsically flawed. His argument is, in outline, that if the meanings of words consisted in a denotative link with objects, then that link would have to be set up by ostensive definition, that is, by indicating an object—typically, by pointing one's finger at it—and uttering its name. This is the view Wittgenstein takes Augustine to hold. But ostension cannot serve as the *foundation* for language-learning because in order to understand that an object is being named the learner would have to be in command of at least part of language already—namely, the language-game of naming objects. The point can be explained like this: suppose you are teaching a non-English speaker the word 'table', and that you do so by uttering the word while ostending (pointing at) a table. Why should he take it that you are naming the object rather than, say, describing its colour, its function, or the polish of its surface—or even ordering him to crawl under it? Of course the language-learner in this example, since he already has command of his own language, may well take it that the language-game in question is that of naming objects; but for a *first-time* learner no such knowledge is available. How then could language begin to be learned if meaning is denoting and thus dependent on ostensive definitions?

What Wittgenstein wishes us to see as a result of his critique of ostensive definition are the following implications: first, that naming is *not*, contrary to the *Tractatus* theory, the basis of meaning, and secondly that the naming relation itself is not simply a matter of ostensively established correlations between sounds (or marks) and objects, but has to be understood in terms of the way names and naming enter into our linguistic activities. The first point is a cautionary one, for in the *Tractatus all* language had been explained in terms of the denotative model, and now in the *Investigations* Wittgenstein is showing that this model simply cannot serve as the paradigm for explaining how the whole of language works—that indeed it is a source of error and perplexity to try to make it so serve. The second point connects with the concept of *meaning as use*; this is a central feature of the *Investigations* and what it involves requires explanation.

There is, deliberately, no *systematic* 'use theory of meaning' in the *Investigations*. Wittgenstein's appeal to the concept of use is intentionally broad for the reason that uses of expressions are as various as the language-games in which they occur, and therefore no single formula can capture their variety. Indeed, there is nothing sacrosanct about the term 'use' itself; Wittgenstein in addition talks of the *functions* of words and sentences (P 11, 17, 274, 556, 559), of their *aims* and *purposes* (for example, P 5, 6, 8, 348), their *offices* (P 402), and of their *roles* and employments (for example, P 66 ff.), intending by these different locutions to capture a general notion of the *part expressions play in language*, the central idea being that mastery of a language consists in being able to employ its expressions in the many different language-games to which they belong. In view of the multiplicity of language-games it is inevitable that the concept of use should in this way be a broad one and that therefore no single formula can be found to encapsulate it. Nor, indeed, should it be treated as a formula itself; the slogan 'meaning is use' is not, for Wittgenstein, a *definition* of meaning. To grasp its full purport one has to understand something more of Wittgenstein's discussion in the *Investigations*, specifically in connection with his views about the relation between *meaning* and *understanding* and his argument that understanding is not an inner mental state or process but 'mastery of a technique' (P 199); and that the technique in question consists in *following the rules* for the use of expressions.

One of these matters was mentioned in the preceding section in connection with Wittgenstein's transitional period. This is that Wittgenstein came to reject the idea that one's *understanding* something by an expression consists in one's going through an inner mental process. Wittgenstein is particularly concerned to reject the notion that in grasping meaning there is something 'lying before one's mind'—a picture or image, as the *Tractatus* suggests; for understanding a word is not an experience like seeing red or feeling a pain (P 140, 154, 217–18). This is not to deny that there might be experiences accompanying understanding—a certain word might evoke an image or, because of memory associations, say, a pleasant feeling—but these do not *constitute* the word's meaning or one's understanding of it. Wittgenstein is here rejecting the empiricist view that meaning is grounded in sensory experience; and for Wittgenstein the consequence of his rejecting this view is that two theses follow; first, that one does not teach the meaning of words by setting up an association in the learner's mind between the word and an experience of some object or situation, and secondly that our attaching meaning to an expression on different occasions of using it does not consist in having the same experience or going through the same mental process each time.

Wittgenstein gives several reasons for rejecting the 'inner state/process' view of understanding. One is that the logic (the 'grammar', as he puts it) of the concepts of meaning and understanding differs from that of experiential concepts. Consider pain: this is an experience, and we can talk of pain lasting for a long or a short time, of being in one's toe or in one's head, of being intense or dull. We cannot say any of these things about understanding an expression; we do not understand an expression for a long time, or in our toes, or intensely. Another reason is that different people associate different images with, or have different reactions to, the same expression; accordingly the meaning of the expression cannot consist in these mental accompaniments, nor can one's understanding of the expression do so (cf. P 137–8). A third reason, and perhaps the most important, is that it is *not enough* for an understanding of an expression that a particular inner mental process should be going on. To illustrate what he means by this Wittgenstein gives the example of one's using the word 'cube', and says that it is a mistake to think that having a mental picture of a cube 'before one's mind' is what one's understanding the word consists in, because the mental picture does not and cannot by itself *tell* one what the word 'cube' means. The mental image of a cube could indeed be associated with any number of expressions—'box', 'sugar', 'geometry', 'whisky on the rocks'—and therefore it does not *dictate* how the word 'cube' is to be correctly understood (P 139–40); we cannot, that is to say, read off from any of the associable images what the word's meaning *is*.

These considerations give rise to another, more general, matter. This is that some philosophers, recognizing the kind of difficulty Wittgenstein is here pointing out, and therefore finding it difficult to identify understanding with *particular* mental processes, have been tempted to think that there is a special kind of *underlying* (and therefore hidden) mental process which constitutes 'grasping the meaning' of an expression—that is, a process which takes all the pictures or associations (or a focal subset of them) which go to make up the meaning of that expression, and combines them, in some way, into something which it is difficult to specify and which, therefore, can only be elicited and inspected by a penetrative philosophical analysis. Wittgenstein rejects this outright; indeed the main target of his attack on the 'inner state/process' conception is the view that understanding is something *hidden*—is not just 'inner' (in the mind) but *deep* in the mind.

Having said what meaning and understanding are not, Wittgenstein proceeds to give a positive account of what they are. Here the concept of understanding is central. Wittgenstein says: 'To understand a sentence means to understand a language. To understand a language means to be master of a technique' (P 199). This says that 'understanding' is *knowing how to do* something; in the case of language, understanding language means *knowing how to use it*. Thus the connection between understanding, meaning, and use is an intimate one. Two immediate implications are these: first, another reason for Wittgenstein's rejection of the 'inner process' conception becomes apparent—it is that this conception offers nothing to explain how we are able to *use* expressions. By contrast the notion of 'understanding', as something we *do*—an ability we exercise, a technique we employ—is directly associated with the notion of use, given that *using* is itself an *activity*. The second implication is that understanding, as a practical capacity, is something that is recognized and measured by *outward* criteria—by the activity people engage in, by how they behave—and therefore, far from being inner or private to the mental life of an individual, it is something which exists out in the open, in the public domain. This has important corollaries, as we shall now see.

3 *Understanding and rule-following*

Wittgenstein's account of language-understanding, where 'understanding' is mastery of a technique or practice in the way just explained, turns on the notion of *following a rule*, the idea being that the practice in which understanding the meaning of expressions consists is that of observing the rules for their use in the different language-games they belong to (note that talk of 'rules' is naturally and intentionally allied to that of 'games'). Wittgenstein's discussion of rule-following occurs mainly in P 143–242. It is not a straightforward matter, and is accordingly the subject of much debate; the following account of it should be read with this in mind.

One way of approaching Wittgenstein's discussion of rule-following is, once again, to recall that part of the *Investigations'* purpose is the negative one of repudiating philosophical attitudes of the kind exemplified in the *Tractatus*. Now, language-use is clearly a rule-governed activity—a 'normative' activity, as philosophers say. The model adopted by Wittgenstein in the *Tractatus* to describe the normative character of language was that of a *calculus*, that is, a structured system of strictly defined rules (the rules of logic) which function automatically. Such a calculus is like a machine which, fed with certain raw materials, manufactures a determinate product in an exact, orderly, and unvarying manner. In the same way, the rules of logic—and therefore, on the *Tractatus* view, the rules of language—have a strict application which determines outcome. In the case of language the outcome is *meaning*: one understands the meaning of an expression when one has mastery of the rules for its use. *This* conception Wittgenstein does not deny in the *Investigations*, of course, for the later philosophy turns on it; what he denies is that the rules in question form a single, rigid underlying system and—even more importantly—that they are in some way *independent of us*, as the *Tractatus* had implied. In other words Wittgenstein rejects the notion of a *calculus* and replaces it with that of a language-game: in the *Tractatus* there is a single, strictly uniform calculus underlying the whole of language; in the *Investigations* there are many different language-games whose 'grammars'—the use-rules—lie open to inspection.

In the *Tractatus*—and in the 'Augustinian' view of language generally—the idea is that the rules for the correct use of a word are in some way determined by the nature of the object denoted by that word, for it is only in this way that the meaning of the word (the denoted object) can govern that word's use. Wittgenstein rejects the denotative theory; this leaves the meaning of the word solely a matter of the rules for its use. But now that there is only the word and its use-rules at stake, it is important not to be misled by the notion of rules itself, for there is a common view about, for example, the rules of logic and mathematics which has it that those rules *dictate* whether or not we are doing something correctly *independently of our practice of applying or following those rules*; and this in Wittgenstein's view is a mistake, not only in itself but because it carries with it the thought that a set of rules constitutes a complete and decisive calculus for a given practice, in the sense that once one has mastered those rules one can read off from them, in an automatic way, the correctness or otherwise of what one does. The model of the rules of logic is in Wittgenstein's view particularly harmful as applied to *language* because there is an enormous diversity of rules governing the use of expressions in language, whereas in logic there is a single, all-embracing and rigid set of rules *constituting* the 'language' in which logic consists.

The calculus conception treats two features of rules and rule-following in a way that gives rise to the problems Wittgenstein wishes us to avoid. One is that in obeying a rule one has the sense of being guided or coerced by the rule; the rule seems to *tell* one what to do, to *dictate* one's activity. The other is that in a calculus like, say, arithmetic the rules determine in advance what outcomes will flow from applying them: for example, it is tempting to think that once I have defined (given the rules governing) the ten numbers 0–9, the operations of addition and subtraction, and the relation of equality, the whole of arithmetic automatically follows—it is as if every arithmetical truth (and falsehood) is already 'contained' in, or settled by, those basic rules. Accordingly, it seems that there is something inexorable about the rules which makes the correctness or otherwise of what I do wholly independent of my doing it. (Each member of a class of schoolchildren might add up a column of figures using different procedures—some in their heads, some on their fingers, others with a calculator or an abacus—but there will be a uniquely right answer at which those who follow the relevant arithmetical rules correctly will arrive; and this answer was the right one *before* they began adding.)

A problem with the notion of rule-following is that on the one hand the *feeling* of being guided by a rule does not guarantee that the rule *is* being followed, for someone might think he is following a rule but in fact be applying it incorrectly; while on the other hand someone's acting in accordance with a rule may be a merely coincidental matter—that person might not be *following* the rule at all; he might, for example, even be ignorant of its existence. Yet both the guiding function of rules, and the fact that observance of them constitutes *doing things correctly* in whatever activity is at issue, appear to be essential to the very notion of rules and rule-following. Accordingly, says Wittgenstein, espousers of the calculus conception attempt to explain these features, and to surmount the problems associated with them, by looking for a unitary account of what underlies rule-following, typically by thinking of rule-following as an inner mental process; and further, by giving this account in terms of some sort of mental *mechanism*—more than likely, a *causal* one. All of this is, says Wittgenstein, a mistake; his reasons, once again, are those he advances against the attempt to give a unitary account of anything to do with meaning and understanding, still more one which proceeds in terms of 'inner' and 'hidden' processes of mind.

These strictures apply more to that feature of rule-following which involves the subjective sense one has of rules being coercive or action-guiding. The other feature mentioned—the apparent 'independence' of rules—suggests, Wittgenstein says, the spurious view that rules somehow give rise to *objectivity*. The arithmetical example well demonstrates what this means: as noted, the rules of arithmetic seem to settle, *in advance*, what is right and what is wrong in the results of our applying them. Thus there is a uniquely correct answer to the arithmetical question '$56,897 + 54,214 = ?$', and this answer is in a sense *there*, settled by what the rules permit even before we work the calculation. We check the correctness of our application of the rules by determining what they (the rules) say; the standards of correctness imposed by the rules thus appear to be external to our observance of them because they are not dependent on our activity of applying them for what they determine as correct.

The two features of rules upon which the calculus view concentrates are, of course, related: it is the externality or 'objectivity' of the rules which gives us the sense of being led or guided by them. Together these two features give rise to the presumption that rules are like railway lines along which we move in a fixed direction (P 218) or like a machine which works in a determined and determining way (P 193–4). Wittgenstein's objection is not to the fact that rules are *guiding* or constitutive of *correctness*; rather, his objection is to the 'railway track' or 'machine' models themselves, on the grounds that they turn the concept of guidance, as we have seen, into that of coercion, and the concept of a standard of correctness into that of something 'external and objective'. What Wittgenstein emphasizes is the crucial fact that what *constitutes* a rule is *our collective use of it*; rule-following is a general practice established by agreement, custom, and training. Therefore, although rules indeed guide us and afford us with our measures of correctness, they are not independent of us and hence do not constitute a coercive standard imposed from outside our rule-following practices themselves. Wittgenstein gives us an example: consider a signpost such as one might find at a crossroads or on a footpath. The signpost tells one what direction to take, but not because it coerces one to go there; its guiding function rests upon the fact that there is a custom, a practice, which establishes the use we make of signposts in general and our understanding of what that function is. And this is just what we are to understand by 'rule' in the case of language—'A rule stands there like a signpost' (P 85, cf. P 198).

The key notion here is that of a 'custom'. Wittgenstein says 'a person goes by a signpost only in so far as there exists a regular use of signposts, a custom' (P 198); 'The application of the concept "following a rule" presupposes a custom' (R, p. 322). By employing the notion of a custom (he elsewhere uses the expressions 'institution', 'use', 'practice' to mean the same thing) Wittgenstein intends to make a number of points, two of which are especially important. One is the by now familiar claim that, in opposition to the view of the calculus theory, rule-following is not an inner mental activity, something hidden, but is a public matter; when someone sees a signpost and goes in the direction it indicates, he is not internally obeying a rule and then—as a second step which follows causally or in some related way from the first 'internal' step of obeying—behaving in accordance with it: his taking the direction indicated by the signpost *just is* his following the relevant rule. Rule-following is not therefore a mysterious activity at all; it *shows* itself in our practice, it is *manifest*. To understand rules and rule-following we have only to remind ourselves of what is familiar in all our many different kinds of normative behaviour (playing chess, cooking from a recipe, doing arithmetic, and so on, as well as using language in all the many different kinds of language-games there are). The other point is that rule-following is essentially a social practice, that is, something which exists in a community; and that it is the existence of *agreement* in the community which establishes the rules we follow: Wittgenstein says, 'The word "agreement" and the word "rule" are *related* to one another, they are cousins. If I teach anyone the use of the one word, he learns the use of the other with it' (P 224). The fact that rule-following is essentially a community-based activity entails that nothing can count as a 'private' observance of a rule—there cannot be a Robinson Crusoe who lays down and thereafter observes a certain rule, for such a person could not know from one occasion to the next that he was indeed observing the rule—he may well *think* that he was doing so, but he has no means of checking. Whether someone is following a rule or not depends upon the availability of public criteria for his doing so: 'And hence also "obeying a rule" is a practice. And to *think* one is obeying a rule is not to obey a rule. Hence it is not possible to obey a rule "privately": otherwise thinking one was obeying a rule would be the same thing as obeying it' (P 202). (The notions of privacy and 'criteria' are important ones for Wittgenstein and I revert to them below.)

In addition to insisting on the essentially communal nature of rules and rule-following based on agreement, Wittgenstein insists that the idea of a 'custom' be taken literally, as something regular, repeated, established. He says: 'The application of the concept "following a rule" presupposes a custom. Hence it would be nonsense to say: just once in the history of the world someone followed a rule (or a signpost; played a game, uttered a sentence, or understood one; and so on)' (R, pp. 322–3).

Since rules rest on the agreed and accepted practices of a community, they are, says Wittgenstein, their own justification. There is no extrinsic or objective factor present in rule-following other than the constraint which lies in the fact that one is *not* following a given rule if one's activity fails to conform to the community's practice in that case. This separates Wittgenstein's view from the *Tractatus* conception of there being something—the world, the facts—set over against language and constituting the objective restraint on it; in the *Investigations* his view is that it is a mistake to look for some form of external justification or grounding for our practices. The justification or grounding is in our practices themselves; in a related connection Wittgenstein says, 'Giving grounds . . . comes to an end . . . the end . . . is our *acting*, which lies at the bottom of the language-game' (OC 204). This enables him to say further that following a rule is something we do unreflectively (R, p. 422) or even blindly: 'When I obey a rule, I do not choose. I obey the rule *blindly*' (P 219). What he means can be grasped by considering, say, chess; there is no answer to the question 'Why does the king move only one square at a time?', for if it is *chess* one is playing then that simply *is* the rule. In effect, therefore, Wittgenstein's view is that rule-following is an habitual practice, one in which we are trained as juvenile members of our linguistic community: 'Following a rule is analogous to obeying an order. We are trained to do so' (P 206). He puts this point more explicitly in the *Blue and Brown Books* (p. 77): 'The child learns this language from the grown-ups by being trained to its use. I am using the word "trained" in a way strictly analogous to that in which we talk of an animal being trained to do certain things.'

4 'Forms of life', private language, and criteria

Taking the considerations of the preceding two sections together, we can describe Wittgenstein's theory of meaning and understanding as follows. The meaning of an expression is what we understand when we understand that expression. Understanding consists in knowing the expression's use across the variety of language-games in which it occurs. Knowing its use is having an ability: the ability to follow the rules for its use in those different language-games. Rule-following is not a mysterious inner process of grasping something like a calculus which objectively imposes standards of correctness; rather, it is a practice embedded in the customs and agreements of a community and as such is essentially public. Rules do indeed guide and provide standards of correctness—but they do so because they are based on agreement; to follow a rule correctly is to conform to the established practices of the community. We acquire the ability to use expressions—to follow the rules for their use—by our training as members of that community.

This summary is intended to bring out the connections between the notions of meaning, understanding, use, rules, and their basis in agreement within a community of language-users. But one should not take it to imply that it is possible to understand expressions *individually*, for in Wittgenstein's view it makes no sense to say that someone understands just one or a few sentences, or that he follows just one or a few rules. To understand any given sentence is to understand the language-games of which it is part; correlatively, to follow a rule is to have mastery of the *practice* of rule-following itself.

One immediate problem that suggests itself in Wittgenstein's account of meaning and understanding is that if the use-rules for a language are the product of agreement among members of the linguistic community, with no external objective restraints on that usage in the shape of 'the facts' or 'the world', does it follow that *truth* is the product of our agreements also? Wittgenstein is aware of this problem and has a response: ' "So are you saying that human agreement decides what is true and what is false?"—It is what human beings *say* that is true and false; and they agree in the *language* they use. That is not an agreement in opinions but in *form of life'* (P 241, emphasis added).

This concept of 'forms of life' plays an important part in Wittgenstein's later philosophy, for it is the notion he appeals to whenever his enquiry reaches a point at which other philosophers would be tempted to begin looking for deeper or more fundamental justifications for the concepts deployed in our thought and talk. What Wittgenstein means by a 'form of life' is this: it is the underlying consensus of linguistic and non-linguistic behaviour, assumptions, practices, traditions, and natural propensities which humans, as social beings, share with one another, and which is therefore presupposed in the language they use; language is woven into that pattern of human activity and character, and meaning is conferred on its expressions by the shared outlook and nature of its users (cf. P 19, 23, 241, P II, pp. 174, 226). Thus a form of life consists in the community's concordance of natural and linguistic responses, which issue in agreement in definitions and judgements and therefore behaviour. Because the 'foundation', so to speak, of the practices which language-use consists in is the form of life into which that language is woven, it follows for Wittgenstein that questions about the ultimate explanation or justification of the concepts embodied in our thought and talk very soon *come to an end*—what justifies our usages is the shared form of life underlying them, and that is that: no more either need be or indeed can be said. The form of life is the frame of reference we learn to work within when trained in the language of our community; learning that language is thus learning the outlook, assumptions, and practices with which that language is inseparably bound and from which its expressions get their meaning. And this is why explanation and justification neither need to nor can go beyond a gesture towards the form of life: 'If I have exhausted the justification I have reached bedrock, and my spade is turned. Then I am inclined to say: "This is simply what I do" ' (P 217); 'What has to be accepted, the given is—so one could say—forms of life' (P II, p. 226).

The notion of a form of life is closely connected with what Wittgenstein insists is the *essentially* public character of language, a theme in the later philosophy which appears, as we have seen, in his rejection of the idea that meaning and understanding—and hence rule-following—are 'inner', 'hidden' states or processes of mind. Wittgenstein advances an argument in this connection which has not so far been mentioned but which has assumed great importance in the literature on the *Investigations*. This is the 'Private Language Argument', the burden of which is that there can be no such thing as a language invented by and intelligible to a single individual only. That this is so follows immediately from Wittgenstein's view that language is *essentially* public, a view he maintains because of all the considerations discussed above; but in P 243–363 Wittgenstein gives the private language question an extended treatment for an important additional reason. This is that in the tradition of philosophy beginning with Descartes it is held that the starting-point for all knowledge and explanation lies in our direct acquaintance with our own experience and states of mind. Thus Descartes's starting-point is the 'I think' recognition of which guarantees 'I exist'; for the empiricists it is sensory experience and our reflection upon it which provides the basis for our beliefs about the existence of external things and other minds. On these views a private language is eminently possible, for they permit the thought (in some cases, they *start from* the thought) of a Robinson-Crusoe-from-birth who constructs a language by means of private, inner ostensive definitions linking words with experiences. In a related way, the idea of a private language is implicated in our standard conception of how we come to have in our language expressions referring to our own pains, moods, feelings, and the rest, given that these are private to us: no one else can have access to such states unless their possessors give expression to them in language or behaviour; no one else can experience *my* moods or pains, or even detect their existence if I do not wish it. Since this is so we come to think that we 'name' our sensations by means of an inner ostension, as though when we have a stomach-ache we 'point inwards' and say 'this is a stomach-ache'. And this suggests that an individual could construct a language for speaking to himself about his sensations and inner life which is *in principle* closed to everyone else—the 'in principle' means that such a language is not merely a secret code which no one else as a matter of fact understands but which *could* be cracked, like the Enigma code or Pepys's *Diary*, but which *cannot* be understood by anyone other than its speaker: a language, in short, which is *logically* private to its speaker.

It is against this conception—of a *logically* private language—that Wittgenstein inveighs in the sections of the *Investigations* mentioned. The primary reason has already been given: to understand a language is to be able to follow the rules for its use, and nothing can count as private rule-following for otherwise there would be no distinction between following a rule and merely *thinking*—perhaps mistakenly—that one is following a rule (P 202). But there are other reasons. For Wittgenstein, to speak a language is, as we have seen, to participate in a form of life; coming to share a form of life consists in being trained to share it; such training obviously has to take place in public, for otherwise it is not a training in the *sharing* of the form of life which gives meaning to language (cf. P 244, 257, 283). From this it follows that both 'private' experience and the language we use to speak of it are in fact neither of them *private*; there are and have to be *public criteria* for the application of expressions about pain, moods, and the rest, in order for there to be such expressions at all. One way to make this clear, Wittgenstein says, is to consider how we use the word 'pain' in talking of ourselves. On the view he rejects, 'pain' is the name of a certain kind of sensation, and we come to give that name to that kind of sensation by an act of inner ostension. But ostensive definition, as we saw above, is something that works only in the context of a previously understood convention or language-game in which pointing, uttering a sound, and so on, are recognized by the participants to constitute the process of attaching a denoting label to some item. There can be no such previously established language-game here. Since 'pain' is not linked with the relevant kind of sensation by ostension, it does not *denote* at all; 'pain' is not a label. How then is it connected with the sensations we use it to talk about? Wittgenstein says that 'one possibility' is that *talk* of pain is a learned substitute for the groaning and wincing which is the *natural expression* of pain (P 245, 256–7); 'A child has hurt himself and he cries; and then adults talk to him and teach him exclamations and, later, sentences' (P 244). The idea is that what we typically think of as private states and processes—pain, anger, and the rest—are features of our human nature which therefore have natural expressions in behaviour (a baby, for example, is able to inform us of its pain and rage by means other than language), and that the linguistic devices we use to talk of them are publicly learned replacements for that behaviour.

This view establishes a link between how we use talk of pain in our own cases and how we use it to talk about others' pain. On one traditional view, the way we come to think of ourselves as having justification, in appropriate circumstances, for ascribing pain or kindred 'inner' states to others, is by analogy with our own cases: if I prick my finger and it bleeds and I groan, inwardly feeling pain, then if someone else pricks his finger, bleeds, and groans, I infer that he must inwardly be feeling pain likewise. But this argument—it is called 'the argument from analogy'—is a weak one; it does not logically guarantee the inference I draw to the other's inner states, for he might be dissimulating or acting, or may even be a cleverly contrived robot which feels nothing. This is the source of scepticism about other minds: how given that the 'argument from analogy' does not work, can I claim to be justified in believing that there are any minds other than my own in the universe? Wittgenstein's view constitutes an answer to this problem. The rules for the use of 'pain' and other psychological expressions, he says, are public ones, which apply equally when the talk is of myself or of others; there are not two sets of rules for such expressions, one governing self-ascription and the other governing other-ascription of the states in question. Consequently, my grounds for saying that someone else is in pain are afforded by his behaviour together with my grasp of the rules for using the word 'pain'.

This view is not to be understood as a straightforward 'behaviourist' theory of the kind which says that the meaning of 'pain' *just is* the set of bodily signs in which wincing and groaning consist. Rather, Wittgenstein says, these signs are 'criteria' for application of the word 'pain'; what I *also* know about such behaviour is that it can be pretence, dissimulation, and so on. Understanding this is part of understanding pain-talk. But given this understanding, the way such behaviour enters into the web of our activities and practices, and the relation of these to our nature, tells me when it is appropriate to say that another is in pain (and also when to say 'this is a case of pretence' and the like).

Wittgenstein's notion of a 'criterion' has attracted much discussion. It is the notion of a species of justification or warrant for employing expressions, a warrant which lies half-way between deductive and inductive grounds for the use of expressions. What this means can be explained in the following way. 'Deductive grounds' are those which would *entail* or *conclusively settle* that use of a given expression is demanded whenever those grounds are present, for the reason that those grounds exhaustively constitute the sense of that expression. An example of this view is the crude behaviourism just mentioned; an espouser of such a view would take the fact that someone winces and groans to entail that he is in pain. But this is far too strong a theory, for in identifying the grounds for saying 'he is in pain' with the meaning of 'pain' the deductivist overlooks those other considerations, such as pretence and the rest, which show that the meaning of the word cannot be *defined* as the grounds for its application.

By contrast, 'inductive grounds' are those in which someone's wincing and groaning count as mere symptoms or clues on the basis of which it might be inferred that he is in pain. Such clues will not themselves be part of the *meaning* of the word 'pain', however, which on the inductivist view is something denoted by 'pain'—something private and hidden in that person's subjectivity—namely, the inner, private *feeling* of pain. On the inductivist's view the link between wincing and groaning, on the one hand, and the inner experience of pain, on the other, is a merely contingent one.

Wittgenstein's talk of criteria, as noted, is designed to fall between these two views. Our understanding of the part played by wincing and groaning (the behavioural signs) in manifesting pain is, he says, part of our grasp of the *meaning* of the word 'pain'—such signs are not merely contingent symptoms of pain—but at the same time they are not deductive grounds for ascribing pain to someone who winces and groans, because our understanding of 'pain' also comprehends those cases where such behaviour is *not* a manifestation of pain. In short, the criteria for ascribing pain are given by the language-game of which pain-ascriptions are a part, and it is the practice of experiencing, recognizing, and talking about pain which we learn when we learn how to use the word 'pain'.

Discussion of the private language question and the issue of pain, moods, and other putatively private mental states takes us into the realm of Wittgenstein's philosophy of mind or, as it is often called, his 'philosophical psychology'. What Wittgenstein has to say in this connection is a very important corollary of his views about meaning and understanding—in the opinion of some commentators it is indeed the *basis* of his philosophy of language—and it is necessary therefore to consider them a little further, as follows.

5 *Mind and knowledge*

In the *Tractatus* Wittgenstein dismisses 'psychological questions', among which he includes questions about experience and knowledge, as 'empirical' and therefore as part not of philosophy but of science. For this reason he barely mentions such matters in the *Tractatus*. In the later philosophy, in sharp contrast, they occupy centre stage along with the discussion of meaning. It is entirely natural that they should do so, given Wittgenstein's concern to argue that understanding the meaning of expressions in language does not consist in private mental states or processes; for his view implies that there is something wrong not just with this way of thinking about understanding but with the very idea of 'private mental states' *in general*. Accordingly, starting with *The Blue Book* but chiefly in the *Investigations, Zettel*, and elsewhere among the later writings, Wittgenstein attacks the idea that the concepts of experience, thought, feeling, intention, expectation, and the rest, are concepts of what is inner and private, accessible only to the individual who possesses them.

It was mentioned earlier that the view Wittgenstein is attacking is one which has been dominant in the history of philosophy since Descartes. This view accords to subjective experience a peculiar primacy and importance. It says that what we are directly acquainted with are our own private states of mind, about whose contents and character, because of their immediacy, we have completely certain knowledge; and these states, including among them sensory experiences, afford us with the starting-point of all our knowledge and belief not just about ourselves but about everything outside ourselves also—chiefly, the external world and other minds. In Descartes's philosophy the starting-point is the *ego*, of whose existence one cannot help but be certain; for the empiricists it is sensory experience which serves as the incorrigible basis for our beliefs about the world. On this conception first-person knowledge of psychological states is wholly unproblematic, whereas third-person knowledge of them is quite otherwise; the reason is that detecting such states in others—even, indeed, being justified in taking it that such states exist outside oneself—is at best a matter of inference from the intrinsically unreliable clues afforded by the overt signs, behaviour, and so on, which others manifest.

In attacking this Cartesian thesis Wittgenstein inverts the order of difficulty: it is not the question of third-person ascriptions of psychological states which is problematic, he says, for such ascriptions work on the relatively straight-forward basis of public criteria for the use of psychological terms, as described above in connection with 'pain'. Rather, what needs investigation is the *first-person* case, for it is here, Wittgenstein says, that a fundamental mistake is being made by Descartes and others in the philosophical tradition; namely, that first-person ascriptions of psychological states ('I have a pain', 'I expect that . . .', 'I hope that . . .', 'I intend to . . .') are *reports* or *descriptions* of essentially private inner goings-on. Wittgenstein denies that these locutions are any such thing, and argues instead that they are *manifestations* or *expressions* forming part of the behaviour to which the psychological concepts at issue apply. The key concept here is that of 'expression'.

What Wittgenstein means by 'expression' is set out in his investigation of first-person talk of pain. At P 244, already quoted in part, he says '. . . how does a human being learn the meaning of the names of sensations?—of the word "pain" for example. Here is one possibility: words are connected with the primitive, the natural expressions of the sensation and used in their place. A child has hurt himself and cries; and then adults talk to him and teach him exclamations and, later, sentences. They teach the child new pain-behaviour.' Wittgenstein's claim is that someone's saying 'I am in pain' is a *manifestation* of his pain; it is not an outer sign of something else which is occurring internally, but is itself part of his pain-behaviour. It is an expression of pain in the way that groaning and wincing are expressions of pain, but it is a learned substitute for those more primitive expressions. Despite the phrase 'here is one possibility' in the quotation given above, which suggests that first-person psychological talk might be understood in other ways too, Wittgenstein applies this conception of 'expression' across the board. Of wishing, expecting, and remembering—to take just three examples from the whole range of psychological concepts—Wittgenstein says: 'By nature and a particular training . . . we are disposed to give spontaneous expression to wishes in certain circumstances' (P 441); 'The statement "I am expecting a bang at any moment" is an *expression* of expectation' (P 253); 'The words with which I express my memory are my memory reaction' (P 343). Thus, sometimes part of what it is to wish for something is to say 'I wish . . .', and sometimes part of what it is to expect something is to say 'I am expecting . . .'. Expectation can be expressed in other ways too; one might feel tense, or pace up and down, or look at one's watch often; but saying 'I am expecting . . .' is not something different from such behaviour—neither, still less, is it a report or description of it—it is *part* of it. Of course the verbal behaviour is, because learned, more complex than the 'primitive' behaviour in which pacing up and down consists; Wittgenstein takes the view that a command of language introduces levels of richness and subtlety unavailable to non-language-using creatures: 'A dog believes his master is at the door. But can he also believe his master will come the day after tomorrow?' (P II, p. 174). But the difference between verbal behaviour and the other behaviour is one of degree, not of kind; verbal behaviour is an extension of the natural expressions of expectation, pain, and so on, which take the form of pacing or wincing as the case may be.

Wittgenstein's reason for thinking this way about psychological concepts is of course that the meaning of words like 'pain', 'expectation', and the rest cannot be fixed by private inner ostension, a point established, in Wittgenstein's view, by the private language argument. Rather, like all words, their meaning is their use, and their use is settled by the publicly agreed rules for their use in the shared form of life upon which the possibility of that agreement rests. Accordingly, the application of psychological terms is uniform; there is not one set of rules for third-person applications and another for first-person applications. The rules are the same and turn on the same public criteria; 'nothing is hidden'. In just the way therefore that first-person ascriptions of psychological terms turn on their being expressions of pain, expectation, or whatever, and therefore parts of pain, etc., behaviour itself, so third-person ascriptions of them are expressions of our behaviour *towards others*: 'Being sure that someone is in pain, doubting whether he is, and so on, are so many natural, instinctive kinds of behaviour towards other human beings, and our language is merely an auxiliary to, and further extension of, this relation. Our language-game is an extension of the primitive behaviour. (For our *language-game* is behaviour)' (Z 545). And this means in Wittgenstein's view that there is no sceptical problem about 'other minds' of the kind which has dogged philosophy since Descartes, because the considerations just mentioned—dealing with the public criteria constituting the sense of psychological terms and therefore our warrant for their use—show that *all* states thought of as *essentially* 'inner' by traditional philosophers have, and must have, outer criteria; and that one can, in a quite ordinary and unmysterious way, literally just *look and see* what state someone is in: 'Consciousness in another's face. Look into someone else's face, and see the consciousness in it, and a particular *shade* of consciousness. You see on it, in it, joy, indifference, interest, excitement, torpor, and so on . . . Do you look into *yourself* in order to recognize the fury in *his* face? It is there as clearly as in your own breast' (Z 220); 'Consciousness is as clear in his face and behaviour, as in myself' (Z 221); ' "We *see* emotion"—as opposed to what?— We do not see facial contortions and make inferences from them (like a doctor framing a diagnosis) to joy, grief, boredom. We describe a face immediately as sad, radiant, bored, even when we are unable to give any other description of the features.—Grief, we would like to say, is personified in the face. This belongs to the concept of emotion' (Z 225).

A major corollary of all these points is, for Wittgenstein, that they force us to reconsider another extremely important philosophical concept, namely that of *knowledge*. In the tradition of philosophy it was held that the special primacy of our acquaintance with our own psychological states furnishes the foundation for whatever else we can come to know or at least believe with justification; for on the traditional view we *know* with certainty the content of our own thoughts, experiences, and so on, but have to draw more or less doubtful inferences from these to whatever lies outside them. Wittgenstein argues, in opposition to this view, that the use thus being made of the concept of knowledge is wholly mistaken, for the reason that we can only *know* what it makes sense to *doubt*, and that since whenever one is in pain or expects to hear a bang one cannot doubt *that* one is in pain or expects to hear a bang, one therefore cannot claim to *know* that one is in pain or has that expectation. This point is best illustrated by looking at Wittgenstein's response to certain theses advanced by G. E. Moore on the subject of knowledge and certainty.

In a well-known paper entitled 'Proof of an External World' Moore argues that there are a number of propositions which he can know with utter certainty to be true. One is that he has two hands; the 'proof' (if one is needed) is, he says, that he can hold his hands aloft and display them. And there are therefore many other such propositions which can be known with equal certainty. Moore is here alluding critically to Descartes's claim in the *Meditations* that whereas one can be certain, whenever one thinks of it, of one's own existence as a 'thinking thing' (a mind), it can legitimately be doubted whether one has 'hands and a body' (*Meditations* I). In Moore's 'common-sense' philosophy such doubts are refutable with the greatest ease; proof that there are hands is as simple a matter as displaying them. Wittgenstein, although siding with the tenor of Moore's down-to-earth rejection of Cartesian views on knowledge and doubt, argues that both Moore and Descartes are mistaken in their thinking about these concepts. His reason, as indicated, is that it is senseless to lay claim to knowledge where doubt itself is senseless; since in all but rare and unfortunate circumstances the question whether one has hands simply does not and cannot sensibly arise, the assertion 'I know that I have hands' therefore involves a misuse of 'know'. Wittgenstein's case for this turns on considerations about the nature of doubt and his view of what constitutes the 'foundations' of our ordinary knowledge and our daily life. These considerations are as follows.

Doubt, Wittgenstein says, is itself possible only in the context of a language-game. If doubt concerning whether I have hands is to be intelligible, then I must understand what is meant by talk of 'hands' and of my 'having' them. But then this understanding, since it is based upon the language-game which makes it possible, itself rules out the meaningfulness of having such doubts; for to have them is to threaten the very conditions for the meaningfulness of the words being used: 'The fact that I use the word "hand" and all the other words in my sentence without a second thought, indeed that I should stand before the abyss if I wanted so much as to try to doubt their meanings—shews that absence of doubt belongs to the essence of the language-game' (C 370). A language-game, it is to be remembered, is a form of life; it is a practice or a set of practices involving agreement about the rules for the use of words. From Wittgenstein's familiar claim that 'Our talk gets its meaning from the rest of our proceedings' (C 224) it follows that 'If you are not certain of any fact, you cannot be certain of the meanings of your words either' (C 114). This means that not only does doubt about one's having hands, except in very unusual circumstances, make no sense *within* the language-game, but also that the language-game itself cannot be called into question *as a whole* or from 'outside': the language-game, as a form of life, is 'the given'. Wittgenstein points out that a child who is learning, say, history has to accept the language-game before he can question whether something is true or whether something exists (C 310–15); 'Doubt', he says, 'comes *after* belief' (C160). If the pupil continually doubted whether the world had existed for longer than a few hours or years, the business of learning history would be impossible. Wittgenstein says that such doubts are 'hollow' (C 312), for in effect they try to make the entire language-game itself impossible. But if the language-game were impossible then the doubt itself would fail to make sense: 'A doubt that doubted everything would not be a doubt' (C 450).

What is being ruled out by these considerations is doubt concerning matters which are fundamental to our linguistic and other practices. Wittgenstein is not saying that there cannot be *any* doubt about anything, for of course there can be.

95

But legitimate doubt can only make sense in the context of a framework which is itself not a subject for doubt: 'The game of doubting itself presupposes certainty' (C 115). Moore's claim about his hands—and by extension any claim about basic matters of fact concerning the existence of material things, the continuous history of the world, and so on—are therefore not legitimate subjects for doubt because they constitute the frame of reference for all our practices. Wittgenstein says: 'My *life* consists in my being content to accept many things' (C 344); 'My life shews that I know or am certain that there is a chair over there, or a door, and so on' (C 7). Accordingly, Moore—and the (Cartesian) philosophical tradition whose outlook informs Moore's approach to these matters—is in Wittgenstein's view mistaken in failing to see that he does not and cannot *know* what he claims to know: 'I should like to say: Moore does not *know* what he asserts he knows, but it stands fast for him, as also for me; regarding it as absolutely solid is part of our *method* of doubt and enquiry' (C 151); 'When Moore says he *knows* such and such, he is really enumerating a lot of empirical propositions which we affirm without special testing; propositions, that is, which have a peculiar logical role in the system of our empirical propositions' (C 136).

The idea of 'testing' and of the 'peculiar logical role' of certain propositions echoes what Wittgenstein elsewhere says in the later writings about the connected facts that having reasons, and giving justifications, has to end somewhere. Where they end is the form of life constituting the language-game; this is the framework which confers intelligibility on what we do. Testing our beliefs can only be carried out against a background of beliefs which are not open to test: 'the *questions* that we raise and our *doubts* depend on the fact that some of our propositions are exempt from doubt, are as it were like hinges on which those turn' (C 341). The exempt propositions are the 'grammatical' propositions, that is, the propositions constituting the framework of our language and practices, and they form the system within which all testing takes place (C 83, 90–2, 105). The beliefs expressed by these propositions are variously described by Wittgenstein to illustrate the fundamental role they play; he says that our commitment to them is part of our nature (C 359), that their 'special role in our frame of reference' (C 83) consists in their being the 'substratum' (C 162) or 'scaffolding' (C 211) of our ordinary testable beliefs.

Although Wittgenstein talks of these beliefs as constituting the 'foundation' (C 401, 411, 415) of our language-games he does not mean by this expression what philosophers normally mean by it. Typically the conception of 'foundational beliefs' is taken to mean beliefs which are fixed and permanent; thus some philosophers claim that there are beliefs which are logically necessary conditions for *anything* that can count as thought or experience, such that even Martians or a divinity would have to have them if they were to enjoy anything recognizable as experience. Wittgenstein, rather, has it that the foundational beliefs are only *relatively* foundational—they are like the bed and banks of a river which determine the course along which the waters flow (C 96–9); the bed and banks are in course of time eroded and therefore shift, but this is a long process and from the viewpoint of our ordinary talk and practice the foundational beliefs serve as what is 'fast' and 'solid' (C 151). But the important point is that the foundational role of the 'grammatical' propositions consists in their indubitability in *practice*, in *action*: 'it belongs to the logic of our scientific investigations that certain things are *in deed* not doubted' (C 342).

The upshot of Wittgenstein's investigation of doubt and certainty is captured in the rhetorical question 'Can one say: "Where there is no doubt there is no knowledge either"?' (C 121). And this is intended to undermine the Cartesian view that first-person knowledge is *knowledge*, hence supporting Wittgenstein's attack on the view that privilege attaches to the private mental states in which philosophers have located the source not just of knowledge but of meaning and understanding. Although the account just given of Wittgenstein's reflections on knowledge is drawn from *On Certainty*, which has a later and more developed view of these issues than occurs in the *Investigations*, the fundamentals of this view are present in the rest of the later philosophy, wherever Wittgenstein's concern is to show that psychological concepts do not apply to something essentially private. This is shown by a dialogue with himself which he sets out in the *Investigations*:

In what sense are my sensations *private*?—Well, only I can know whether I am really in pain; another person can only surmise it.—In one way this is false, and in another way nonsense. If we are using the word 'to know' as it is normally used (and how else are we to use it?), then other people very often know when I am in pain.—Yes, but all the same not with the certainty that I know it myself!—It can't be said of me at all (except as a joke) that I *know* I am in pain. What is it supposed to mean—except perhaps that I *am* in pain? (P 246)

6 *Some reflections and comments*

The preceding sections show that Wittgenstein's later philosophy is an elaborate edifice of interconnecting themes. Nevertheless, its basic intention is clear, and the key concepts in terms of which it is expressed—use, rules, language-games, and so on—are so prominent in all the later writings (including those on the foundations of mathematics) that there is no difficulty in identifying them and seeing, in rough terms, what work they are designed to do. I shall now reflect briefly on Wittgenstein's enterprise in the later philosophy and on the concepts central to it. Many points of detail invite comment, but I shall confine the discussion to some strategic remarks about Wittgenstein's main points only.

One thing that immediately strikes a critical reader of the later works is that the chief concepts occurring in them are either vague or metaphorical or both. The idea of 'games' is a metaphor; the talk of 'use' and 'forms of life' is unspecific. This of course is deliberate; Wittgenstein's method was to avoid systematic theorizing, and to insist instead upon the *variety* of language, his motive being to escape the pitfalls, exemplified by the *Tractatus*, of erecting a rigidly monolithic theory of language and thought which succeeds only in falsifying the issues or at best oversimplifying them. But a reader of the later philosophy might nevertheless suspect that Wittgenstein, in his anxiety to repudiate a monolithic approach, has veered to the opposite exreme; in place of the single fixed structure unearthed in the early philosophy there is substituted a great patchwork of practices so diverse that, Wittgenstein claims, no systematic account can be given of what meaning and understanding consist in (whereas a systematic account of what they do *not* consist in, namely any species of private mental state or process, *is* in his view possible). One might agree with Wittgenstein that it is a mistake to look for the kind of theory offered by the *Tractatus*; but it does not follow that *no* systematic account can be given of language, for it is plausible to except that when what is under consideration is a connected and patterned set of practices—whether it is riding a bicycle or speaking a language which is in question—it should be possible to formulate a theoretical representation (to give an account, provide a description, even an explanation) of what is involved. Nothing Wittgenstein says persuades one that such a task is pointless or impossible. On the contrary, Wittgenstein himself seems to have done just that with his talk of rules, language-games, and the rest, despite his official disclaimers about giving a positive theory. But his account is highly general, and in the crucial respects therefore too vague; one feels that our understanding of the matters discussed would have been advanced further if Wittgenstein had given his notions more precise content, and ventured to say how he thought they applied in practice.

One important criticism of the later philosophy might be that a generalized appeal to notions like 'use' and 'rule-following'—especially since in Wittgenstein's view what is meant by 'use' and 'rule-following' varies widely according to context—tells us dissatisfyingly little. This reservation can be made more explicit if one takes, as an example, a consideration of how much one learns from being advised to think of *meaning* as *use*.

First it is necessary to note that the concept of 'use' is itself a various one. One can talk of *how* something is used, of what it is used *for*, of *when* its use is appropriate, and even of what it is used *in* (as when one says: 'lard is used in baking'). On the first two heads, one can say, for example, of a hammer that *how* it is used is by grasping the handle and aiming the flat surface of its head at the target, and—quite differently—that what it is used *for* is driving in nails, flattening surfaces, calling meetings to attention, and so on. Such explanations tell us something about hammers, although they do not uniquely determine that it is *hammers* we are talking about—there are other things whose handles we grasp (golf-clubs, suitcases) or which can be used for driving in nails (the heel of a shoe, a stone). It is clear enough that one can talk of the uses of words in an analogous way, as Wittgenstein suggests; one can explain how a word is used, when its use is appropriate, and what kind of work it can be used to do. But in what sense will such explanations be explanations of *meaning*? Suppose I tell you *how* a word was used: if I say it was used effectively, or insolently, or musingly, I say nothing about its meaning. Suppose I tell you what a given word can be used *for*: if I say it can be used to insult, to appease, to inspire, I still say nothing about its meaning.

These comments suggest that the connection between meaning and use is neither so close nor so obvious as Wittgenstein's remarks sometimes imply. Unquestionably it would be a mistake to commit oneself to the strong doctrine that meaning and use are the *same*. This is shown by the fact that one can know the meaning of a word, in a perfectly standard sense of this phrase, without knowing its use, and one can know its use without knowing its meaning. For example, one can know that the Latin word *jejunus* means 'hungry' without knowing how to use it in a sentence; and, conversely, one may know how to use the expressions 'amen' and 'QED' without knowing their meanings. Moreover, many words have uses *without* meanings—personal names, prepositions, conjunctions, and the like, are cases in point. Use therefore can by no means be the whole story about meaning; it may be part of that story, but it does not exhaust whatever it is meaning consists in. Moreover, to say that use is part of the story is not by itself much help—at best it is only a beginning; for what it is one knows, or is able to do, which constitutes one's capacity to use expressions is not suggested by the concept of use itself; one has to look further afield (or deeper).

The appeal to use as a key concept in the later philosophy is primarily intended by Wittgenstein to focus attention on *what words are used to do*, since an account of this, in Wittgenstein's view, is (in some not wholly clear way) tantamount to an account of meaning itself. One way of assessing this crucial idea is to note that in the period during which the impact of Wittgenstein's thought on philosophy was at its most immediate, this conception was intimately involved in discussion of what was called the 'speech-act' aspect of language use. Consider *what is being done* in the use of these expressions: 'Stop!', 'Where is it?', 'It's on the table.' The first is an order, the second a question, the third a statement—and ordering, questioning, stating are actions we perform in our use of language: hence 'speech-acts'. There are many others—promising, appraising, criticizing, commending, and joking are examples. The idea is that showing how an expression is used to perform a speech-act tells us about the meaning of that expression. So, for example, it is suggested, in a much-discussed theory of moral discourse, that the word 'good' functions in the speech-acts of commending and evaluating, which permits us to say that we explain the meaning of 'good' when we explain that it is *used* to commend or to place a positive valuation on something. Likewise it has been suggested that we grasp the meaning of the word 'true' by noting that it is used to confirm, support, admit, or agree with something that has been stated. These proposals might appear to lend greater exactness and therefore greater plausibility to Wittgenstein's own vaguer view, but once again they do not prove to be satisfactory. Showing why helps to explain the unease one feels about unqualified appeals to the notion of use.

Consider the claim that 'good' is used to perform the speech-act of commending. If someone says, 'This is a good pen', then clearly he is commending the pen. But if someone asks, 'Is this a good pen?', equally clearly, even though the occurrence of 'good' is literal, no commending is going on. A defender of the speech-act theory might respond by saying that 'good' is not *invariably* used to commend, but that its presence in utterances typically shows that the speech-act of commending is 'in the offing', so that 'Is this a good pen?' can be construed as having the force of 'Do you commend this pen?' But even this will not do, for in such sentences as 'I wonder if this is a good pen', 'I don't know whether it's a good pen', 'I hope it's a good pen', commendation is irrelevant to the case, which is proved by the fact that one is *not* saying 'I wonder if I commend this pen?', 'I hope I commend this pen', and so on.

These thoughts suggest that it is a mistake to suppose that reminding ourselves of the main uses of words like 'good' and 'true' is *enough*, by itself, to settle any questions we might have about the meaning of those terms. Indeed, it is notoriously the case that questions about goodness and truth, which are paradigmatically large philosophical questions, cannot be resolved simply by noting the ways 'good' and 'true' are as a matter of fact used in common parlance—that is, in the language-games in which they typically occur. It would seem to be an implication of Wittgenstein's views that if we 'remind' ourselves of these uses, philosophical puzzlement about goodness and truth will vanish. This is far from being so.

These remarks indicate one reason why the vagueness of Wittgenstein's key concepts—in this case *use*—might generate dissatisfaction with his later philosophy. Another reason is that this feature of Wittgenstein's ideas actually invites rather than solves familiar philosophical difficulties, some of them very problematic. For one example, what we sometimes appear to be given by the later philosophy is a picture of language—more accurately, the patchwork of heterogeneous practices in which language is involved—as somehow autonomous, as though language floats free of anything like an objective reality—a world—in a way wholly different from what is proposed in the *Tractatus*, with its picture of a realm of independent facts on the one hand, faced on the other hand by language (thought), with the former constraining and determining the latter, and with truth and falsity consisting respectively in a correspondence or lack of it between the two structures. In the later philosophy, by contrast, the suggestion sometimes appears to be that the world is dependent upon the 'form of life' of which language is part; at very least, there is no question of the correct use of language being decided by something *independent* of language—we do not go right or wrong in language use according to whether we correctly or otherwise describe objective facts, but rather according to whether we follow the mutually agreed and observed rules of our linguistic community. The community as a whole cannot go right or wrong either; it just *goes*; the only constraints on use are the internal ones founded on agreement and custom. Provided that changes in use were systematic across the whole community, no change would—because no change *could*—be detected; the community might co-operatively be veering in its application of rules, whether in progressive or in arbitrary ways, and this would be unknown and anyway irrelevant. Indeed, these very remarks would be meaningless, for they presuppose some point of vantage from which comparisons could be made—but such a viewpoint, since it would have to be external to the form of life, is impossible.

It is not easy to see, from a scrutiny of Wittgenstein's texts, what we are to make of this. Most Wittgensteinians deny that the later philosophy constitutes a form of 'anti-realism', but at the same time it appears that Wittgenstein himself thinks that the most one can say on the question of an independently existing reality is that our language-games—more generally, our practices—in which we deal with things like, say, chairs, tables, and the rest, *presuppose* a commitment on our part to there being such a reality. This comes out in the view, expressed in *On Certainty*, that the validity of many beliefs consists in the role they play in language; the very sense of our talk about an external world, in which there are hands or in which physical things have existed for a long time, turns on our unquestioning acceptance of such beliefs themselves as (here we have more metaphors) the 'bed and banks' or 'scaffolding' of that language-game itself. Wittgenstein puts this point by saying that propositions like 'physical objects exist' are 'grammatical'—that is, *logical*—propositions, having a special role in our discourse as forming part of its very conditions of meaningfulness. Likewise, religious discourse is a language-game in which talk of God similarly plays a fundamental role, and consequently the validity of religious discourse is something internal to itself (a point some theologians have gratefully accepted from Wittgenstein because it helps them defend against the criticism that no independent means exist for substantiating religious claims). There is no question of asking, still less answering, questions about the validity of these language-games as a whole, or *from without*; they rest upon 'the form of life'—the shared experience, the agreement, the customs, the rules—which underlie them and give them their content. Accordingly it appears that, in Wittgenstein's view, language and thought are in some sense internally self-determining and self-constituting, and that therefore reality is not, as he had thought of it in the *Tractatus*, independent of language and thought.

The problems such a view creates are many. One is that if we accept some such view we are obliged to explain what *appears* to us, in our ordinary experience of it, to be the independent character of the world. Why, if there is no genuinely independent world constraining the way we act, think, and talk, does it seem as if there *is* one? Why does it at least seem as though our practices and thought have always to accommodate themselves to something intractable and separate? The fact that the world appears to exist independently of us can indeed be explained by anti-realist theories, even by those strong versions which have it that thought or experience is the determiner of what exists. But the *details* of such a theory are extremely important, since on them turns the theory's very acceptability. If therefore Wittgenstein is committed to the view that reality is not independent of language and thought, he has but does not fulfil a responsibility to say something more about why our experience and beliefs are so trenchantly realist in character.

Another and allied problem which arises from these of Wittgenstein's views is that they sometimes appear to commit him to *relativism*. This is a point which interests anthropologists as well as philosophers, and in part explains the former's interest in Wittgenstein. What is involved can be explained as follows.

There are, broadly speaking, two kinds of relativism, 'cultural' and 'cognitive'. Cultural relativism is the thesis that there are differences between cultures or societies, or between different phases in the history of a single culture or society, in respect of social, moral and religious practices and values. For example, one among the things which distinguishes contemporary Western society from, say, Indian society is the markedly different set of practices followed in courtship and marriage. In the latter marriages are arranged, and the parties to them meet only once or twice, very briefly and in the company of their families, before the marriage ceremony. In the West courtship is left to chance as to its inception and individual preference as to its continuation and outcome. It is evident that the institution of marriage has different significances in these two societies.

Cultural relativism is not philosophically problematic, for it is clear that our being able to recognize cultural differences of the kind described presupposes an ability on our part to gain access to other cultures so that we can recognize the differences *as* differences; which shows that there are points in common between cultures which allow mutual access and hence mutual understanding to take place.

Cognitive relativism is a quite different matter. It is the view that there are different ways of perceiving and thinking about the world or experience, ways possibly so different that members of one conceptual community cannot at all grasp what it is like to be a member of another conceptual community. Some philosophers argue that with respect to any culture other than our own, or even with respect to an earlier phase in our own culture's history, we can never have more than an indeterminate grasp, at best, of what it is like to be a member of it. This is because, they argue, any view of the world is a highly theoretical and interpretative matter, and our efforts to make intelligible to ourselves an alien world-view—an alien conceptual scheme, or 'form of life' as Wittgenstein would say—will inevitably proceed in terms of our *re*-interpreting the aliens' concepts, beliefs, and practices into our own terms, which is the only way that we, from our own standpoint, can make any sense of them. On this view it is possible and even likely that there are conceptual schemes so utterly different from our own that we cannot regognize their existence—or if we can, that nevertheless they are quite sealed off from our capacity to get an inkling of what they are like from within. One thing that immediately follows from cognitive relativism is of course that truth, reality, knowledge, moral value, and the like, are *our* truth, *our* reality, and so on; they are not absolute but relative—they are parochial to us, even to the slice of history we happen to occupy; and that therefore there are as many versions of 'truth', 'reality', and 'value' as there are different conceptual schemes or 'forms of life'.

Wittgenstein sometimes appears to be committed to cognitive relativism as just described. He says: 'If a lion could talk, we could not understand him' (P II, p. 223); 'We don't understand Chinese gestures any more than Chinese sentences' (Z 219). These remarks suggest relativism across 'forms of life'; Wittgenstein may be saying that because meaning and understanding are based upon participation in a form of life, and because the forms of life in which, in their different ways, lions and Chinese engage are quite different from ours, it follows that we cannot understand them— their view of things is inaccessible to us and vice versa. In *On Certainty* Wittgenstein appears to commit himself to relativism in a single form of life across time, by saying that our own language-games and beliefs change (C 65, 96–7, 256), which entails that the outlook of our forebears might be as inaccessible to us cognitively as is that of the lions or, differently again, the Chinese.

Cognitive relativism is a troubling thesis. Consider the point that it makes the concepts of truth, reality, and value a matter of what sharers in a form of life happen to make of them at a particular time and place, with other forms of life at other times and places giving rise to different, perhaps utterly different or even contrary, conceptions of them. In effect this means that the concepts in question are not concepts of *truth* and the rest, as we usually wish to understand them, but concepts of opinion and belief. We are, if cognitive relativism is true (but what does 'true' now mean?) in error if we think that 'truth' and 'knowledge' have the meanings we standardly attach to them, for there is only *relative* truth, there is only reality as *we*, in *this* conceptual community at *this* period in its history, conceive it.

The reading of Wittgenstein which suggests that he takes such a view is consistent with much of what he otherwise says.

For Wittgenstein the meaning of expressions consists in the use we make of them, that use being governed by the rules agreed among the sharers of a form of life. This presumably applies to expressions like 'true' and 'real' themselves—indeed, it is precisely Wittgenstein's point that such expressions cease to be philosophically significant once we remind ourselves of their ordinary employments. It follows that the possibility of there being other forms of life—even just one other—with different agreements and rules, means therefore that each form of life confers its own meaning on 'true' and 'real'—and therefore truth and reality are relative not absolute conceptions. This is a highly consequential claim.

From some of what Wittgenstein says—particularly about 'natural expression', that is, the way people are apt to feel and act as a result of their human nature—we might be led to suppose that all *human* communities share the same form of life, and hence that truth is human truth, reality human reality. The form of relativism to which Wittgenstein is committed might, that is, simply be anthropocentrism. This interpretation is supported by his saying that 'the common behaviour of mankind is the system of reference by means of which we interpret an unknown language' (P 206, cf. 207). But the remark about the Chinese (and see also Z 350), which conflicts with the remark just quoted, seems to propose a more radical relativism than that; consistently with one interpretation admitted by the notion of a 'form of life' Wittgenstein's view might be that cognitive relativities follow the same demarcation lines as cultural relativities. This would be an extreme relativism indeed.

One need not take as one's target so radical a form of the thesis to show that cognitive relativism is unacceptable, however. This can be demonstrated as follows. Suppose that cognitive relativism is the case. How then do we recognize another form of life *as* another form of life? The ability to detect that something is a form of life and that it differs from our own surely demands that there be a *means* for us to identify its presence and to specify what distinguishes it from ours. But such means are unavailable if the other form of life is impenetrable to us, that is, if it is closed against our attempts to interpret it enough to say that it is a form of life. This means that if we are to talk of 'other forms of life' at all we must be able to recognize them as such; we must be able to recognize the existence of behaviour and patterns of practices which go to make up a form of life in which there is agreement among the participants by reference to which their practices can go on. Moreover, if we are to see that the form of life is *different* from our own we have to be able to *recognize* the differences; this is possible only if we can interpret enough of the other form of life to make those differences apparent. And therefore there has to be sufficient common ground between the two forms of life to permit such interpretation. This common ground has to involve two related matters: first, we have to share with the aliens some natural capacities and responses of a perceptual and cognitive type, giving rise to at least some similar beliefs about the world; and secondly we have to be able to share with them certain principles governing those beliefs; for one important example, that what is believed and therefore acted upon is held to be *true*. This has to be so because, as remarked, detecting *differences* is only possible against a shared background; if *everything* were different participants in one form of life could not even begin to surmise the existence of the other.

But this requirement for mutual accessibility between forms of life gives the lie to cognitive relativism. This is because the respects in which 'different' forms of life share an experiential and conceptual basis which permits mutual accessibility between them are precisely the respects in which those forms of life are *not cognitively relative at all*. Indeed, cultural relativism, which is not just an unexceptionable but an important thesis, itself only makes sense if there is mutual accessibility between cultures at the cognitive level. Hence it would appear that the only intelligible kind of relativism there can be is cultural relativism.

Wittgenstein's relativism, or at least the relativism that sometimes seems to be implied by his views, makes no distinction between the cultural and cognitive types. Indeed, he barely seems to be aware of relativism as a possible—and unacceptable—implication of some of his remarks, and particularly of his 'forms of life' notion. Yet that notion underwrites the whole of the later philosophy, as the 'given' or 'bedrock' which provides the ultimate basis for meaning, use, rules, knowledge, and the psychological concepts. Therefore both the intrinsic vagueness of that notion, and its unacceptable entailment or apparent entailment of relativism, raise a question mark over his later philosophy as a whole.

The foregoing discussions concern general points in Wittgenstein's philosophy. I turn now to a more particular matter: Wittgenstein's discussion of rule-following and private language. This constitutes the most central and important aspect of his later philosophy. But here too there are problems, the chief of which is that these of Wittgenstein's views contain an inconsistency. This can be demonstrated as follows.

Wittgenstein's argument against private language is standardly taken to be an argument against the possibility of *logically* private language, that is, language which only a single individual *can* know. This allows that there can be *contingently* private languages, languages which in fact only one person knows but which could be understood by others—which are, in short, translatable into public languages. Sometimes it is thought that an example of a contingently private language would be, say, Pepys's *Diary*; but this is merely a public language in cypher, and does not constitute a philosophically interesting case of privacy. A better example might be a language invented by someone solitary from birth—a lifelong Robinson Crusoe. Such a language would be private in an interesting sense, but it would be only contingently private because it would admit of being understood by others. On Wittgenstein's view Robinson's language only counts as a *language* because it admits of being publicly understood.

The commentator's insistence that Wittgenstein intended to rule out logical but not contingent privacy arises from the fact that the conception of contingently private language seems to be perfectly in order; it is widely recognized that such languages are possible and that it would be difficult to argue otherwise.

When we look at Wittgenstein's remarks on rule-following,

however, it turns out that he is committing himself to something different from, and much stronger than, the claim that there cannot be logically private languages. What the rule-following considerations entail is that *language is essentially public*. The argument for this, to recapitulate, is that language-use is a rule-governed activity, and that rules are constituted by agreement within a language community (only within such a community can one succeed in following rules, since otherwise one could not distinguish between following a rule and only thinking one is doing so; and where such a distinction is unavailable there is no rule-following and hence no language). But then if language-use is a rule-following activity, and such activity is essentially a matter of public agreement, as Wittgenstein argues, it follows that language is essentially—that is, *logically*—public.

And here is the problem for Wittgenstein: if language is logically public there cannot be languages which are in *any* sense private. There cannot be a Robinson-Crusoe-from-birth who invents and uses even a contingently private language, because on the rule-following argument he could not, since he is not a member of a linguistic community, distinguish between following a rule and only thinking he is doing so, and hence could not be using a language at all.

Indeed there is a further, allied, reason why on Wittgenstein's principles there cannot be contingently private language. This is that such a language could not get started. This follows from what Wittgenstein says, as noted in preceding sections, about language learning, which demands a public setting in which the tyro can be trained in the practices (centrally, the rule-followings) of his linguistic community. For a Robinson-Crusoe-from-birth there can be no such beginning, and therefore—on Wittgenstein's views—no language.

The conflict apparent in Wittgenstein's views, then, lies between the strong claim that language is logically public, and the weaker claim that there cannot be logically private language. The former rules out, while the latter allows, that there can be contingently private languages. Wittgenstein advocates the former when specifically discussing rules, and the latter when specifically discussing private language. However, for his overall position the rule-following considerations and all they involve (agreement, the language-community, and so on) are fundamental. Accordingly, it would seem that, when a choice is forced, the strong thesis is the one to which Wittgenstein must adhere, thereby rejecting the weaker. But then the price is commitment to the debatable thesis that there cannot be contingently private language. (The other alternative—abandoning the stronger thesis—is not open to Wittgenstein; if he took it he would be giving up what is crucial to his later philosophy.)

These difficulties in Wittgenstein's position remind one that the rule-following and privacy issues give rise to yet another serious problem. The problem has already been mentioned: it concerns the fact that if rules are constituted by agreement within a language community, and are not determined by anything external to that community's practices, then the problem facing a putative private language-user—namely, that he cannot tell whether he is, or only *thinks* he is, following a rule—also faces the community as a whole. How does the *community* tell whether it is following a rule? The answer Wittgenstein gives is: it cannot tell. This admission is the nub of the problem. If, in the case of the individual, nothing counts as marking this crucial difference, then according to Wittgenstein the individual is not following rules at all, and hence is not using language. But does this not apply to the language-community as a whole? And if it does, then the paradoxical result would seem to be that the language-community does not use language.

In recent discussions of Wittgenstein efforts have been made to resolve these and other difficulties. As they stand they are serious and radically undermine Wittgenstein's views. Taken together with the more general criticisms sketched above, they suggest that Wittgenstein's later philosophy is not as it stands persuasive.

4 Wittgenstein and recent philosophy

A. J. Kenny describes Wittgenstein as 'the most significant thinker of the [twentieth] century'. G. H. von Wright considers him to be 'one of the greatest and most influential philosophers of our time'. An opponent of Wittgenstein's views, J. N. Findlay, characterizes him as a thinker of 'immense consequence and originality . . . profound . . . brilliant'. Similar assertions abound in the literature of Wittgenstein.

Anyone reading these large claims would naturally surmise that Wittgenstein is the most influential presence in twentieth-century philosophy. In fact he is not. The quickest way to explain this is to point out that apart from work done by Wittgenstein's relatively small band of disciples, *most* of what has happened in philosophy during and since his time consists exactly in what his writings proscribe: namely, systematic investigation of the very 'problems of philosophy' which he says will vanish when one attends properly to language. The fact is that the majority of recent and contemporary analytic philosophers simply disagree with this claim. Their practice shows that, far from accepting Wittgenstein's outlook, they are more influenced by the philosophical legacy of Frege and Russell than by him. For that among other reasons they remain in the mainstream philosophical tradition which Wittgenstein sought to repudiate. This is a significant matter for understanding Wittgenstein's place in current philosophy, for, as we have seen in preceding chapters, his rejection of the philosophical tradition is expressed as a rejection of what that tradition specifies and defines as the problems of philosophy. That all but his own disciples disagree with him on this central issue is an indication of the fact that Wittgenstein's effect on recent philosophy has been very much less than the claims made by Kenny, von Wright, and others imply.

To say this is not, however, to offer an opposing estimation of Wittgenstein's place in philosophy. It is too soon to judge whether Wittgenstein ranks among those major figures—for example, Aristotle, Locke, Kant—whose place in the history of philosophy is assured because of the value attached to their work by later generations. The reason is the obvious one that it is difficult to make accurate historical judgements about recent and living philosophers. When one surveys the history of philosophy one sees half a dozen thinkers whose stature is, from our point of view, enormous; in their company are a dozen more whose influence and importance endure. This is a select company. It is easy to forget that many others wrote and taught philosophy, some of whom were famous in their time and after it, yet whose reputations have not survived. One example is Malebranche, the French priest of the late seventeenth and early eighteenth centuries, who in his day was celebrated throughout the intellectual world a[nd wh]ose work inspired a large literature in emulation and o[...] Locke devoted a monograph to him; the young [...] [e]agerly sought to meet him when visiting Paris. The w[...] [L]ocke and Berkeley continue to be studied, whereas [...] [Ma]le-branche have fallen into obscurity. Less dram[...] can be drawn from among those figures gener[...] but little read, except by a few scholars or follow[...] drawn at random and perhaps tendentious, a[...] Plotinus, Aquinas, and Schopenhauer. For all [...] and esteem enjoyed by these thinkers in the [...] during a period after their deaths, it would ha[...] then—as the event shows—to presume on the ju[...] history concerning whether they would acquire and [...] the status of truly major figures. And even the reputati[...] major figures at times fluctuate, with periods of obsc[...] intermitting their fame.

These considerations must weigh here. Remarks ab[out] Wittgenstein's place in philosophy can, if they are to have any value, relate only to the period since his death; and for the reasons suggested 'they can furnish no guide to what importance future thinkers may attach to his work. In trying to characterize Wittgenstein's place, then, it is best to leave aside judgements of the kind at issue above, and to proceed as far as possible factually.

There are certain complications in describing Wittgenstein's place in recent philosophy. They result chiefly from Wittgenstein's secretiveness and hesitance about his later thought. This was because he was anxious not to have his ideas disseminated until he had perfected them, and even more anxious not to have them imitated or stolen. Accordingly, he wished to publish them before anyone else did; but he could never feel quite ready to do so, and hesitated so long that in the end all his later work was published posthumously. Two things therefore require explanation: one is the connection between Wittgenstein's views and those of his contemporaries and near-contemporaries who were, like himself, philosophically interested in language; and the other is the way a small but distinctive 'Wittgensteinian school' arose in his lifetime and has flourished since.

For parts of the 1930s and 1940s Wittgenstein was teaching and writing in Cambridge, as we have seen, and some of his writings had a confined publication in the form of typescript copies. Inevitably, by agency of his pupils and the circulation of these typescripts, some of his ideas reached the philosophical community at large. Traces of them—but only traces—can be detected in the work of Gilbert Ryle, J. L. Austin, and certain others. So-called 'Ordinary Language Philosophy', which flourished at Oxford mainly during the 1950s and which is chiefly associated with Austin, is sometimes thought to be a result of Wittgenstein's teachings, but in fact his influence was far less immediate than that; certainly Austin did not take himself to owe his ideas to Wittgenstein. There is no doubt that Wittgenstein's views had some part in promoting the philosophical concern for language which was dominant in the mid-century, even if only in part and at second or third-hand; but it is equally certain that Wittgenstein would have found aspects of 'Ordinary Language Philosophy' uncongenial. None of the people who at that time were prominent in philosophy (in addition to Ryle and Austin there were, for example, Moore, Broad, Russell, and Ayer) were Wittgensteinians; most of them were largely unaffected by Wittgenstein's later ideas, and some were actively hostile to them.

Wittgenstein's influence on his philosophical contemporaries was, accordingly, diffuse and limited. The fact that a 'Wittgensteinian school' came into existence might therefore seem puzzling, but it is explained by the fact that Wittgenstein made ardent disciples of some of his pupils at Cambridge, and in the interval since his death those pupils have, by a kind of apostolic succession, ordained yet other disciples. The Wittgensteinians accordingly make a distinctive although relatively small group in contemporary philosophy, studying Wittgenstein's texts closely and applying his methods, with some of them refusing to take more recent developments in philosophy seriously on the grounds that they involve departures from Wittgenstein's ideas. A considerable amount has been published by these followers, ranging from exegesis to hagiography, and including some original work which has variously been controversial and stimulating.

What is most important, for present purposes, is the continuing response given to Wittgenstein's thought by the philosophical community at large. Here matters are straightforward. There is, as noted above, no question of there being general or even widespread agreement with Wittgenstein's fundamental claims. Rather, the philosophical community responds to Wittgenstein's work as it does to any work in which interesting ideas are offered: it profits where profit is to be had, and differs where it does not agree. Some of Wittgenstein's ideas have accordingly passed into the general currency of philosophical discussion. Much of what Wittgenstein says about meaning in the later philosophy has failed to persuade, although acceptance of the general (and, as it stands, imprecise) thought that *use* is an important part of meaning is widespread, and Wittgenstein's work has had a large part in disseminating it. Where the philosophical community has taken most profit is in Wittgenstein's philosophy of mind. With respect both to meaning and mind Wittgenstein's concern was, centrally, to deny that words mean by *denoting*, by standing for *things*, which had been his view—adopted from Russell and others—in the *Tractatus*. Many philosophers had come to see the error in this view independently of Wittgenstein; where his later philosophy provokes most thought—although by no means always agreement—is in its application of this denial to psychological discourse, having it that there are no hidden or private objects to which psychological terms refer. And in connection with this and the view of meaning which underlies it there are the important matters of rule-following and private language, both of which have provoked much discussion. Many otherwise sympathetic philosophers are cautious in their approach to Wittgenstein on all these questions, however, because of the difficulty which attaches to fixing upon a clear interpretation of what he says; as a result of the obscurities generated by his method and style Wittgenstein's key notions—'criteria', 'language-games', and the rest—are open to different interpretations, and accordingly a *precise* specification of his commitments is difficult to give. It is for this reason that so much of what is published about Wittgenstein consists in attempts at clarification and explanation.

If one were to specify a single reason why few philosophers agree with Wittgenstein's basic outlook it would be that they do not accept his diagnosis of the *source* of philosophical perplexity. Wittgenstein says that problems arise because we misunderstand the workings of our language. He says we are 'bewitched' by language; sometimes, he says, we have an 'urge' to misunderstand it. But this is implausible. Philosophers as various as Plato, Bacon, and Berkeley have enjoined caution over language, and for excellent reasons, some of them mentioned in connection with Russell's views in Chapter 1 above; but to say that *all* philosophical perplexity arises from linguistic misunderstanding is to overstate matters. For one thing, language is an instrument capable of precise use. When it is so used philosophical difficulties can be expressed and investigated clearly. If Wittgenstein's view were right one could sometimes only describe what a given philosophical problem involves if one were sufficiently *careless*. For another thing, attempts to put Wittgenstein's views into practice show that they do not constitute a solution to philosophical difficulties. Wittgenstein says that we should remind ourselves of the ordinary uses of terms in order to 'dissolve' such difficulties. But, as we have seen, attending to the ordinary uses of 'good', 'true', and 'real' does not by itself solve the philosophical perplexities we feel about *goodness*, *truth*, and *reality*. Were matters otherwise, that grateful discovery would have long since been made.

We see, then, that Wittgenstein attracts the plaudits of the commentators, who describe the quality of his mind and work in high, even lavish, terms; yet at the same time he is by no means the key figure in twentieth-century philosophy. There is no paradox here. Broadly speaking there are two measures of a philosopher's importance: one is the amount written about him—a rather crude measure—and the other is the way his ideas determine the content and direction of philosophical discussion in his own time and later. This is a much more accurate measure. On the first criterion Wittgenstein counts as a major figure. But it is only right to note that he is not alone among recent philosophers in having a voluminous literature devoted to him; one thinks of Frege, Russell, and Husserl as subjects of much study. Noting this helps to put the literature on Wittgenstein into perspective. The crucial measure is however the second one. As the foregoing indicates, the content and direction of contemporary philosophy—its problems, its preoccupations, its methods—are not shaped by Wittgenstein's thought. If his work is, as D. F. Pears describes it, 'truly great', then this may change; future generations of philosophers may learn to agree with the claim made by Janik and Toulmin in their *Wittgenstein's Vienna* that analytic philosophers systematically misread and misunderstand Wittgenstein, and they may accordingly come to share with present-day Wittgensteinians a fundamental commitment to his outlook and methods. So far, this has not happened.

I turn, in conclusion, from remarks about the place of Wittgenstein's work in recent philosophy to some even more impressionistic remarks about that work itself.

It needs to be said that many reservations expressed about Wittgenstein's writings are prompted by the interpretational difficulties they generate. These arise because of Wittgenstein's conception of philosophy and his method of doing it. The conception and the method are intimately correlative. As we have seen, philosophy is in Wittgenstein's view a therapy; the point is to dissolve error, not to build explanatory systems. The style is accordingly tailored to the intention. It is vatic, oracular; it consists in short remarks

117

intended to remedy, remind, disabuse. This gives the later writings a patchwork appearance. Often the connections between remarks are unclear. There is a superabundance of metaphor and parable; there are hints, rhetorical questions, pregnant hyphenations; there is a great deal of repetition. Much of this is deliberate—a point often stressed in the foregoing—for Wittgenstein's style is expressly designed to promote his therapeutic objective as against the 'error' of theorizing. Few however would seriously recommend this way of doing philosophy to, say, students. Wittgenstein's method, in the wrong hands, provides excellent cover for charlatanism, since it is *intended* to avoid system and with it the required clarity, rigour, and accuracy which theoretical work demands and which philosophers in general seek. The fact that almost anyone—including people working in subjects other than philosophy—can cull quotations from Wittgenstein's texts for a wide variety of purposes, sometimes opposed ones, should constitute a warning to would-be imitators; to become a resource for aphorism hunters from all quarters is a good indication that one has failed in a major duty: namely, to be clear.

These remarks are premissed on an acceptance of Wittgenstein's own official avowals about therapy and the avoidance of theory. In fact, of course, there *is* a theory in Wittgenstein's later work, as the preceding discussions testify; a theory which can be set out in explicit form, starting from considerations about use and rules and showing how these are ultimately based on agreement in a form of life. The theory has an identifiable structure and content, even if neither, in their turn, are as transparently stated and as fully spelled out as they might be. And a good deal of the difficulty with Wittgenstein's work is that this theory is not presented as such, since it is not officially meant to be there at all—it emerges in bits and pieces, in an *ad hoc* way, and therefore its crucial conceptions are left unclear and often unargued.

The unclarity complained of here as in earlier chapters has, incidentally, been claimed as a virtue of Wittgenstein's work; von Wright says: 'I have sometimes thought that what makes a man's work classic is often just this multiplicity [of possible interpretations], which invites and at the same time resists our craving for a clear understanding.' This is a neat apology for obscurity; one might be forgiven for finding it unpersuasive.

The vividness of Wittgenstein's metaphors, the unexpected examples and turns of thought, generate the sense that something profound is being expressed in his writings. Wittgenstein is in some ways a poet. Once one has sifted his texts and has ceased to be dazzled by the brilliance of metaphor and the poetical quality, one finds much less argument, and very much less definiteness in the crucial conceptions, than is expected in and demanded from philosophical enquiry. This is disappointing. But perhaps the value of Wittgenstein's work lies as much in its poetry, and therefore in its *suggestiveness*, as in its substance. There is no doubt that in this respect Wittgenstein's work has stimulated insights and fresh perspectives, especially in philosophical psychology, which have helped to advance thought about these matters. Work in philosophy which has this effect is always welcome.

Because there can be no question of a detailed estimation of Wittgenstein's contribution here it is perhaps appropriate to conclude with a purely personal one. Like many others, I cannot help being struck by the unusual character of Wittgenstein's writings, which give a strangely original cast even to thoughts and points of view which, in more prosaic dress, are familiar enough. But I find that when one advances beyond the manner and reflects on the content, the irresistible feeling is this: that the journey through Wittgenstein's circuitous, metaphorical, sometimes opaque negations and suggestions is long; but the distance it takes one is short.

Reflection upon the above, together with the memoirs and biographical essays concerning Wittgenstein, suggests a closing thought. Future generations may or may not judge Wittgenstein to be one of the great philosophers. Even if they do not, however, he is sure always to count as one of the great personalities of philosophy. From our perspective it is easy to mistake one for the other; which he is time will tell.

Further reading

Wittgenstein's chief works are as follows (I give them in the approximate order of their composition; the dates given are dates of first publication):

Notebooks 1914–16, ed. G. H. von Wright and G. E. M. Anscombe (Blackwell, 1961).

Prototractatus (an early version of the *Tractatus*), ed. B. McGuinness, G. Nyberg, G. H. von Wright (Routledge and Kegan Paul, 1971).

Tractatus Logio-Philosophicus, trans. D. F. Pears and B. McGuinness (Routledge and Kegan Paul, 1961).

Philosophical Remarks, ed. R. Rhees (Blackwell, 1964).

Philosophical Grammar, ed. R. Rhees (Blackwell, 1969).

The Blue and Brown Books, ed. R. Rhees (Blackwell, 1958).

Lectures on the Foundations of Mathematics, ed. C. Diamond (Harvester Press, 1976).

Remarks on the Foundations of Mathematics, ed. G. H. von Wright, R. Rhees, G. E. M. Anscombe (Blackwell 1956, revised ed. 1978).

Philosophical Investigations, ed. G. E. M. Anscombe and R. Rhees (Blackwell, 1953).

Zettel, ed. G. E. M. Anscombe and G. H. von Wright (Blackwell 1967, revised ed. 1981).

Remarks on the Philosophy of Psychology, 2 vols: vol 1 G. E. M. Anscombe and G. H. von Wright; vol. 2 G. H. von Wright and G. Nyman (Blackwell, 1980).

On Certainty, ed. G. E. M. Anscombe and G. H. von Wright (Blackwell, 1969).

An interesting collection of diary entries, remarks, and apophthegms, culled from notes made by Wittgenstein over several decades of his life, has appeared as *Culture and Value*, translated by P. Winch and selected and arranged by G. H. von Wright (Blackwell, 1980).

The definitive biography of Wittgenstein is *Wittgenstein: A Life* by B. McGuinness (vol. 1 *Young Wittgenstein 1889–1921*, Duckworth, 1988; vol. 2 forthcoming). A biographical essay by G. H. von Wright and a personal memoir by Norman Malcolm are published together as *Ludwig Wittgenstein: A Memoir* (2nd ed. with letters, Oxford University Press, 1984). Further perspectives on Wittgenstein's life, character and work are to be found in Rush Rhees (ed.), *Recollections of Wittgenstein* (Oxford University Press, 1984) and C. G. Luckhardt (ed.), *Wittgenstein: Sources and Perspectives* (Harvester Press, 1979).

Introductions to Wittgenstein's thought are D. F. Pears, *Wittgenstein* (Fontana, 1971) and Anthony Kenny, *Wittgenstein* (Penguin, 1973). Less introductory discussions are provided by R. J. Fogelin, *Wittgenstein* (2nd ed. Routledge, 1987), P. M. S. Hacker, *Insight and Illusion* (Oxford University Press, 2nd ed., 1987) and A. J. Ayer, *Wittgenstein* (Weidenfeld and Nicolson, 1985). For detailed scholarly commentaries on Wittgenstein see M. Black, *A Companion to Wittgenstein's 'Tractatus'* (Cambridge University Press, 1964) and, for the later philosophy, G. P. Baker and P. M. S. Hacker, *Wittgenstein: Understanding and Meaning* (Blackwell, 1980, 1983). A study which has excited much recent debate on crucial aspects of Wittgenstein's thought is S. Kripke, *Wittgenstein on Rules and Private Language* (Blackwell, 1982). For discussion of Wittgenstein's views on the foundations of mathematics— the problem which first attracted him to philosophical work— see Crispin Wright, *Wittgenstein on the Foundations of Mathematics* (Duckworth, 1980) and S. G. Shanker, *Wittgenstein and the Turning-Point in the Philosophy of Mathematics* (Croom Helm, 1987). In Anthony Kenny, *The Legacy of Wittgenstein* (Blackwell, 1984) there is an assessment of Wittgenstein's influence and importance which is different from the one presented here.

For examples of the wider uses sometimes made of Wittgenstein's ideas, in for example theology, anthropology, and political theory, see Fergus Kerr, *Theology After Wittgenstein* (Blackwell, 1986), P. Winch, *Studies in the Philosophy of Wittgenstein* (Routledge and Kegan Paul, 1969), and D. Rubinstein, *Marx and Wittgenstein: Social Praxis and Social Explanation* (Routledge and Kegan Paul, 1981). And for a sample of how Wittgenstein's work is employed by philosophers and literary critics working in the contemporary Continental tradition of thought see H. Staten, *Wittgenstein and Derrida* (Blackwell, 1985).

Index

OXFORD

MORE OXFORD PAPERBACKS

This book is just one of nearly 1000 Oxford Paperbacks currently in print. If you would like details of other Oxford Paperbacks, including titles in the World's Classics, Oxford Reference, Oxford Books, OPUS, Past Masters, Oxford Authors, and Oxford Shakespeare series, please write to:

UK and Europe: Oxford Paperbacks Publicity Manager, Arts and Reference Publicity Department, Oxford University Press, Walton Street, Oxford OX2 6DP.

Customers in UK and Europe will find Oxford Paperbacks available in all good bookshops. But in case of difficulty please send orders to the Cash-with-Order Department, Oxford University Press Distribution Services, Saxon Way West, Corby, Northants NN18 9ES. Tel: 01536 741519; Fax: 01536 746337. Please send a cheque for the total cost of the books, plus £1.75 postage and packing for orders under £20; £2.75 for orders over £20. Customers outside the UK should add 10% of the cost of the books for postage and packing.

USA: Oxford Paperbacks Marketing Manager, Oxford University Press, Inc., 200 Madison Avenue, New York, N.Y. 10016.

Canada: Trade Department, Oxford University Press, 70 Wynford Drive, Don Mills, Ontario M3C 1J9.

Australia: Trade Marketing Manager, Oxford University Press, G.P.O. Box 2784Y, Melbourne 3001, Victoria.

South Africa: Oxford University Press, P.O. Box 1141, Cape Town 8000.

PAST MASTERS

A wide range of unique, short, clear introductions to the lives and work of the world's most influential thinkers. Written by experts, they cover the history of ideas from Aristotle to Wittgenstein. Readers need no previous knowledge of the subject, so they are ideal for students and general readers alike.

Each book takes as its main focus the thought and work of its subject. There is a short section on the life and a final chapter on the legacy and influence of the thinker. A section of further reading helps in further research.

The series continues to grow, and future Past Masters will include **Owen Gingerich** on *Copernicus*, **R G Frey** on *Joseph Butler*, **Bhiku Parekh** on *Gandhi*, **Christopher Taylor** on *Socrates*, **Michael Inwood** on *Heidegger*, and **Peter Ghosh** on *Weber*.

MASTERS

KEYNES

Robert Skidelsky

John Maynard Keynes is a central thinker of the twentieth century. This is the only available short introduction to his life and work.

Keynes's doctrines continue to inspire strong feelings in admirers and detractors alike. This short, engaging study of his life and thought explores the many positive and negative stereotypes and also examines the quality of Keynes's mind, his cultural and social milieu, his ethical and practical philosophy, and his monetary thought. Recent scholarship has significantly altered the treatment and assessment of Keynes's contribution to twentieth-century economic thinking, and the current state of the debate initiated by the Keynesian revolution is discussed in a final chapter on its legacy.

MASTERS

RUSSELL

A. C. Grayling

Bertrand Russell (1872–1970) is one of the most famous and important philosophers of the twentieth century. In this account of his life and work A. C. Grayling introduces both his technical contributions to logic and philosophy, and his wide-ranging views on education, politics, war, and sexual morality. Russell is credited with being one of the prime movers of Analytic Philosophy, and with having played a part in the revolution in social attitudes witnessed throughout the twentieth-century world. This introduction gives a clear survey of Russell's achievements across their whole range.

OPUS

*General Editors: Walter Bodmer,
Christopher Butler, Robert Evans,
John Skorupski*

CLASSICAL THOUGHT

Terence Irwin

Spanning over a thousand years from Homer to Saint Augustine, *Classical Thought* encompasses a vast range of material, in succinct style, while remaining clear and lucid even to those with no philosophical or Classical background.

The major philosophers and philosophical schools are examined—the Presocratics, Socrates, Plato, Aristotle, Stoicism, Epicureanism, Neoplatonism; but other important thinkers, such as Greek tragedians, historians, medical writers, and early Christian writers, are also discussed. The emphasis is naturally on questions of philosophical interest (although the literary and historical background to Classical philosophy is not ignored), and again the scope is broad—ethics, the theory of knowledge, philosophy of mind, philosophical theology. All this is presented in a fully integrated, highly readable text which covers many of the most important areas of ancient thought and in which stress is laid on the variety and continuity of philosophical thinking after Aristotle.

PHILOSOPHY IN OXFORD PAPERBACKS
THE GREAT PHILOSOPHERS
Bryan Magee

Beginning with the death of Socrates in 399, and following the story through the centuries to recent figures such as Bertrand Russell and Wittgenstein, Bryan Magee and fifteen contemporary writers and philosophers provide an accessible and exciting introduction to Western philosophy and its greatest thinkers.

Bryan Magee in conversation with:

A. J. Ayer	John Passmore
Michael Ayers	Anthony Quinton
Miles Burnyeat	John Searle
Frederick Copleston	Peter Singer
Hubert Dreyfus	J. P. Stern
Anthony Kenny	Geoffrey Warnock
Sidney Morgenbesser	Bernard Williams
Martha Nussbaum	

'Magee is to be congratulated . . . anyone who sees the programmes or reads the book will be left in no danger of believing philosophical thinking is unpractical and uninteresting.' Ronald Hayman, *Times Educational Supplement*

'one of the liveliest, fast-paced introductions to philosophy, ancient and modern that one could wish for' *Universe*